Hi! It's Me, Your Dog!

Hi! It's Me, Your Dog!

Let me take you for a walk through my world

by

Emmy-Winning Journalist
Lisa Mendoza

Clovis, California

| Please Note |

This book is not intended to replace professional medical advice for your pet and should only be used to supplement care provided by your veterinarian.

Quill Driver Books/Word Dancer Press, Inc.
8386 North Madsen Avenue
Clovis, California 93611
559-322-5917
FAX 559-322-5967

Printed in the United States
ISBN 1-884956-16-5

Quill Driver Books/Word Dancer Press books may be purchased
at special prices for educational, fund-raising, business or promotional use.
Please contact:
Special Markets
Quill Driver Books/Word Dancer Press, Inc.
8386 North Madsen Avenue
Clovis, CA 93611
1-800-497-4909

To order another copy of this book, please call
1-800-497-4909

Library of Congress Cataloging-in-Publication Data

Mendoza, Lisa 1958-
  Hi! it's me, your dog! : let me take you for a walk through my world /
by Lisa Mendoza.
    p. cm.
  ISBN 1-884956-16-5
  1. Dogs. I. Title.

SF426 .M436 2000

00-040307

TO MY TWO CANINE COMPANIONS THAT ARE HAPPILY WALKING THE PATH OF LIFE WITH ME—LITTLE BOY AND LITTLE GIRL

"The man who has conferred the greatest benefit upon the human race is the primitive savage who first tamed a litter of wolf cubs."

— SIR ROBERT BALL LLD FRS

• Contents •

Old Habits Are Hard to Break

Puppy Power

Is The Doctor In?

My Sex Life

First Class, Please

Kibbles & Tidbits

Happy Birthday To Me!

What I Really Want to Say to You

• *Acknowledgments* •

I'd like to say thank you to the following people: Nancy Clemmensen for sharing her graphic art expertise; my publisher Steve Mettee and editor Dave Marion for their enthusiasm and attention to detail; Kyle Bahre of KB Canine Academy of Stockton, California, Dr. William C. Fellner, DVM, of Hartnell College's veterinarian program, and Dr. Juli Potter of Purdue University's animal behavior department for their careful, thorough, and thoughtful readings of the manuscript and for their valuable suggestions; Michael Snell for his time and input; Anise Luster for sharing her organizational skills; Patrick Speir, for his encouragement and proofreading; Jennifer Speir for her artwork; and the many Central Valley dog lovers who sent me pictures of their beloved canine companions.

• Speaking Out for the First Time •

I Have a Voice!

ey, you! Yes, you…I'm talking to you! Wipe that shocked look off your face. It's just me, your dog. I know you didn't think I could talk, but I can. I just never felt like mentioning it before, because I like the sound of your voice. But now that I've decided to speak, perk up those cute little ears of yours, because I have plenty to share with you. So much, in fact, that I've decided to take you for a little walk through a dog's world. *Don't worry, you don't have to wear a leash.*

But before we get going, I want to take a second to whisper something in your ear, just in case I get hit by a car during our walk. *Hey, the thought horrifies me, too, but it happens.* Are you ready? Come on, move in a little closer. There you go. I *love you. Deeply. Truly. Unconditionally.* Always remember I'm by your side and on your side. What I feel for you is rare in this world. It's lifelong love. *Sentimental, but true.*

Well, now that I've finally gotten that canine confession off my chest, let's begin our walk. I have so much to share with you, and believe me, it's the truth, straight from the dog's mouth. *Come on, let's go!*

"Upbeat" and "outgoing" are words I'd use to describe myself. As a puppy in a cage at an animal shelter, my spirited personality won over the lady who became my new human mom.

I admit I sulk a little when I don't get my way and I confess to turning up my nose sometimes, but I don't think I roll my eyes like my mom says I do. Well... only sometimes!

Since I've lived here, I've learned that there is much to gain by hiding under the tablecloth when the family is eating a meal. The kids don't always keep a good grasp on their food. Heh, heh, heh.

—Robbie

• Let Me Introduce Myself •

Exploring My Mental Ability and Senses

I f you run a background check on me, you'll uncover a little secret. No, I'm not a spy, but I am using the name you've given me only as an alias. You see my real name is *Canis familiaris*. Don't worry, I'm not trying to deceive you by responding when you call me by my alias; it's just that *Canis familiaris* sounds so formal...*and I've certainly never been accused of being a dog who stands on formality.* Even though I don't use my real name, I am proud of it because it links me to my past. Most researchers agree the branches of my family tree, *which, by the way, generations of male members of my family have raised their legs on over the years,* lead back to wolves. Just think, thousands of years ago a primitive man, *who, just between you and me, really needed a shower and a shave,* linked our futures together forever by leaning over and picking up a small wolf cub. *Who would have dreamed of the bond that was to be formed?* Luckily for us, those two were smart enough to realize the union was really a partnership that benefited both of them. Before long they were roaming the wilderness together, hunting for food during the day and huddling around campfires for safety at night.

Boy, have times changed. Now you drive off with a CD blasting, and I stay behind alone in our quiet house, with not even a mouse to chase. If I do go outside, the backyard fence keeps me imprisoned and boredom leads me to spend the day stuffing my face with store-bought dog food. And, while the lonely hours drag on, I struggle to repress most of my natural instincts so you will consider me a "good dog" when you return home.

Don't get me wrong, I'm not complaining; it's just the truth. As a matter of fact, overall, I love our life together, *especially the bacon-flavored dog biscuits you buy me.* But I must admit, I'm often bored and, yes, that's with a capital "B." You see, in the past I spent my time hunting for food, tracking game, catching mice, herding flocks, pulling carts, protecting people and their property, even fighting battles. In other words, I had a job; I earned my keep. Today, I lie around unemployed, looking for things to keep me busy. When I am lucky enough to find something to do, my actions usually land me in trouble and I find myself being disciplined for so-called behavioral and emotional problems. But fortunately, adaptability is my greatest asset. And I believe my most important job lies ahead of me—that of faithful companion who fills your increasingly complex life with love. You have to admit, as this stressful world becomes more and more high-tech, I become better and better for your soul. So the more you know about me, the better for both of us. *To be perfectly honest with you, that's the real reason I think it's time we talked.*

> **"The more you know about me, the better for both of us."**

My Think Tank—My Brain

My brain contains a cerebrum, cerebellum, and brain stem just like yours, but your "think tank" is a little fuller than mine. You have a lot more area set aside in your cerebral cortex for processing thought. What this means is I don't spend my time worrying or contemplating the meaning of life. I just live one moment at a time, enjoying what I can.

My brain allows me to feel a range of emotions. When I hear your car pull into the driveway, I feel happy. When you yell at me, I feel sad. When you leave me alone in an unfamiliar place, I feel scared. When another dog challenges my position, I feel anger. When you signal for me to get in the car, I feel excitement. When you hug me tight, I feel love.

I've noticed humans spend a lot of time trying to figure out how smart I am. I've overheard conversations in which claims are made that I'm brainier than a cat, cow, horse, pig, and almost as smart as a dolphin. I've also heard humans say that Border collies are the smartest dogs and Afghans are the dumbest. Talk like that doesn't ruffle my feathers, because first, I *don't have feathers*, and second some of my best friends are Border collies and some are Afghans and we all get along just fine.

I must admit my intelligence is probably my most misunderstood quality. Sure, on the average I do understand anywhere from 40 to 60 human words, but I hate to break the news to you: human and canine intelligences are just not the same kinds of thing. We're different species, each with our own strengths and weaknesses. In my opinion, what "intelligence" rankings of different dog breeds really do is determine each breed's ability to blend into the human world. I've noticed that researchers who support these rankings like to compare my intelligence to that of a three-year-old child. That comparison doesn't bother me at all. All the three-year-old kids I know explore the world with great curiosity and hearts filled with love. So, as far as I'm concerned, I consider the comparison a compliment.

I admit my brain doesn't enable me to program the VCR, but yours doesn't seem to either. OK, OK, OK, I *know you can do it, you just don't feel like it*! But guess what? I do know enough math to get by. If you don't believe me, try this simple test. Offer me a plate

My name is Ginger, but I think it should be Socrates, because at 15-years-old, I'm a very thoughful dog. As a matter of fact, my personal motto is "cogito, ergo sum." But I also like to chase soap bubbles and run through the hose spray.

—Ginger

with one big juicy steak on it and at the same time offer me a plate with seven big juicy steaks on it. You can bet your last Milkbone I'll bite into the bigger stack first.

In case you're wondering, my brain doesn't completely shut down during all those hours I spend sleeping. I dream, just like you. Some of my dreams are pleasant, some are nightmares. One of my furry friends often cries in her sleep. I've asked her why she does this, but she's clueless. I do know as a puppy she was abandoned. Maybe that's why she has nightmares. As for me, I often dream of running, jumping, and cuddling with you. The dog next door is a typical guy; he snores and dreams of food, sex, and peeing on things.

What's That Smell?—My Nose

Some canine researchers think as much as 40 percent of my brain may be geared toward my olfactory ability. "Olfactory" is a pretty big word. It means "of the sense of smell." I know this because I looked it up in a dictionary I keep in my doghouse. *Yes, it's the one you "misplaced" a couple of months ago.* Well, now that you know I'm a kleptomaniac (*mainly, though, I steal bones and bury them*), you might as well know this extra olfactory brain power is boosted by the fact that I have almost 195 million more "smelling" cells in my nose than the 5 million or so you have in yours. Plus, I have a second smell organ in the roof of my mouth. And, as if that's not enough, my wet nose and the shape of my lips help trap odor molecules. What all this means is that my sense of smell is much more developed than yours. New research shows it may be a million times sharper. I'm happy about that because of all my senses, my sense of smell is the one I rely on the most.

In the canine kingdom, odors do much more than fill the air. They play a crucial role in nearly every aspect of my life. Odors determine everything from where I urinate to where I sleep. Odors also call the shots when it comes to my sex life. Odors even let me know if another dog is a pup and is entitled to favors, such as protection and extra food. For your information, puppies lose their "baby smell"—and their right to extra food—at about three months of age.

It's incredibly important that you understand and respect my sense of smell. It's a vital part of my life. I know I embarrass you when I meet another dog and we begin to do some serious sniffing, but you have to face the fact that dogs do this. We're not being nasty. It's just an instinctive canine greeting behavior. As you've noticed, I also love to sniff anything and everything we encounter while on walks. As long as the object isn't dangerous to me, I really don't see the harm in your letting me take a whiff. I'm just enjoying my keen sense of smell. Please remember that for most humans the world is a visual place, but for me, it's an odor-filled world, bombarded by chemical signals called phero-mones, which are produced by all living things. You visit places; I visit odors. *The downside to this is that I can't keep track of my travels in photo albums like you're able to.*

For years humans have capitalized on my amazing sense of smell and to be perfectly honest with you, I wish it would happen more often. We dogs enjoy sniffing out drugs and explosives stuffed in plastic bags and hidden in virtually every kind of container man can devise. And *let me tell you, I've found illegal stuff in some of the strangest places.* Helping authorities detect harmful agricultural pests is also a lot of fun. Finding termites is entertaining too. *You should try it sometime.* Tracking down missing people is also easy for me because every person, even you, leaves a distinct odor trail. I can even smell the difference between twins.

My highly developed sense of smell also enables me to do such wonderful things as find a pebble after it's thrown over a cliff. I can detect a drop of blood diluted by almost a gallon and a half of water. While these things sound amazing, I can do a lot more. Re-searchers are just now discovering the fact that my nose can de-tect impending epileptic seizures in people. I can also detect changes in the body odor of schizophrenics. I can even smell cer-

I knew something was wrong, but all I could do was hold my human mom close and lick away her tears.
—Nestly

tain cancers in the human body. In the future, I hope humans really put my nose to the test. As far as I'm concerned, the more difficult the challenge, the more rewarding the experience, because I'll be allowed to use the full capabilities of my nose. Remember, when it comes to relying on my senses, I always pick my nose. Let me rephrase that. I always select my nose. *There, that sounds better.*

My amazing sense of smell does have a drawback that you may have noticed. It's common for me to sneeze after being exposed to such things as perfume, cologne, or air freshener. As a general rule of thumb—*I've always wondered why humans use that phrase, which makes about as much sense as saying, as a general rule of paw—anyway, back to what I was saying,* if you can detect an odor, imagine how my nose is being bombarded by it and you'll understand that it won't be long before I sneeze.

I've noticed my nose is a lot longer than yours, but please don't make fun of me. My long nose is beneficial to me. It helps me deal with dust and secondhand smoke a lot better than yours does. A Colorado State University study shows the longer my nose, the less likely I am to develop lung cancer. That's because I have more nostril hair, which is pretty good at filtering the air. B*ut please remember, that's no excuse for anyone to light up.*

Touch the tip of my nose. If I'm healthy, it should typically be clean, smooth, and damp. However, if my diet is lacking in fatty acids and other nutrients, my nose leather may be dry and cracked. T*hanks, but no amount of night cream will help; however, a higher quality dog food containing vitamin E might do the trick.*

What Did You Say?—My Ears

Out maneuvering you when it comes to the nose patrol is just the beginning of my bragging rights. My hearing is also sharper than yours. It's my second most valuable sense.

Just like the outside of your ears, the outside of mine act like radar dishes, but my equipment is much better than yours. Think of it this way, your ears are a science project put together by eighth graders, mine are made by NASA. In case you're wondering, the size and shape of my ears really doesn't matter. Small ears work just as well as big ears. But I must admit that pointy ears, like those of a German shepherd, are a little bit better at capturing sound waves than floppy ears like those of a basset hound.

Want to hear something impressive? I can determine the location of a sound in six one-hundredths of a second. N*ot exactly the speed of light, but it sure leaves your hearing in the dark.* However, before you start feeling inadequate, I must confess my quickness is due to the fact that my ears move independently from one another. Just like Spock's. N*o, not Dr. Spock,* I'm t*alking about the* Star Trek g*uy with the pointy ears.*

I also beat you when it comes to hearing sounds that are farther away. Research shows that if you and I are standing right next to each other, I'll be able to hear sounds that originate more than six times farther away than you can hear. What this means to you is that the next time I suddenly awaken out of a deep sleep and begin growling or barking, don't just yell at me to shut up. You can bet someone or something is in our backyard or alley and you can't hear whoever or whatever it is. I suggest you let me take a look around; as you know, it's better to be on the safe side.

My range of sound is also wider than yours. I can hear subsonic tones that are too low for you to hear and I can also detect sounds that reach as high as 45,000 vibrations per second. Your hearing tops off at 20,000 vibrations per second. By the way, a so-called silent whistle can really drive me nuts. If blown too close to me, it can sound as if a siren is blaring next to my ear. *I'd appreciate it if you would remember this the next time you feel the urge to use one.*

Just like my sense of smell, I wish you'd utilize my sense of hearing more fully. As you may know, dogs have been taught to help hearing-impaired people by signaling when a doorbell chimes or a phone rings, and we're used to locate people who are trapped underground and calling feebly for help. But did you know I can hear thunder long before its rumble strikes your ears, and I may even be able to hear shifting deep in the earth before earthquakes. I'm not suggesting you replace weather stations with Welsh springers or seismographs with schnauzers, but I think more research into my hearing would be a good idea.

I have to admit, there is one thing about my hearing that really puzzles me. You know my hearing is exceptional, but you still choose to yell at me. I can hear you just fine when you use your normal tone of voice. *Really, I can.*

Sometimes I wonder if jealously of my superior hearing triggered the barbaric practice of ear cropping. That's when a dog's ears are intentionally trimmed so they'll stand permanently erect.

Some humans think it makes us look better. *Aren't you glad dogs don't sit around and try to improve the looks of humans?* Ear cropping has been banned by some countries; I hope other nations hear my "yelp for help." *Wow, wouldn't that expression make one serious bumper sticker?*

The Better To See You With—My Eyes

Have you noticed my eyes shine in the dark? Don't worry, I'm not demon-possessed. I have a reflecting layer in each eye. This enables me to see well in dim light, but the downside is that I rarely look my best in photographs.

I want you to know that while I appreciate and value my eyesight, I don't depend on it as much as you depend on your eyesight to get around. My sense of smell and my hearing tell me more about my world than my sight ever will. As a matter of fact, most dogs, except sight hounds, consider sight one of their weaker senses. While dogs are able to see better than humans at night, your sight surpasses mine when it comes to spotting something that isn't moving. I have a tendency to overlook any stationary object, but as soon as it moves, odds are I will spot it before you. By the way, my field of vision is wider than yours. While my range can go as high as 250 degrees, your range is limited to 180 degrees.

Although my eyesight isn't my sharpest sense, it too has benefited man greatly. We dogs have informally helped the blind for at least 2,000 years. But it was the Germans who first trained what we now call seeing-eye dogs. They did it after World War I to help blind soldiers get around. To tell you the truth, it's not difficult to train me. I like to be needed. Take my word for it, a dog trained to assist the blind can do just about anything, even laundry. *It's fun loading and unloading the washing machine, but let me tell you, measuring the detergent is a little tough.*

You've probably read that I'm color-blind. New research shows that's not exactly the case. I see the world mostly in shades of black and white with patches of blue and green—*just like a lot of hippies did in the* 1960s. By the way, please don't feel sorry for me because I've never seen the color purple; as far as I'm concerned the world is still a wonderful and exciting place.

I know you've noticed that I usually avoid eye contact with you. Most humans consider eye contact a good thing, but that's not necessarily the case in the canine world. Usually when a dog stares at another dog in its pack, it's challenging its position. So, since I consider myself lower than you in the pecking order, when I avoid eye contact with you, I'm just being respectful. So don't worry the next time I don't look you in the eye. Remember, it's nothing personal, it's just a dog thing.

I'll Have My Steak Rare, Please—My Taste Buds

You beat me hands down when it comes to the sense of taste. That's because you have six times as many taste buds as I do. The next time you bite into some cheesy, meaty lasagna remember the wide range of flavors you're lucky enough to experience is a blessing I'll never truly know. As far as my taste buds go, food falls in the following three categories: tasty, tolerable, and terrible. You can easily see what category a food is in by how quickly I wolf it down.

Here's a tasty tidbit. While your sense of taste is superior to mine, I enjoy eating just as much as you do. As a matter of fact, I love to eat. It's one of my favorite pastimes. I'm omnivorous just like you—that means I eat a wide variety of foods, but I must confess, I like to consider myself carnivorous. *That's because* I *crave meat.* I know your doctor has encouraged you to cut back on the stuff, but what's sometimes bad for you, can be good for me.

My body is set up for meat consumption. If you could put on x-ray sunglasses and take a peek inside my system, you'd see a simple stomach and short intestines, both designed to digest the red stuff. My system also enables me to put cholesterol on the list of things I really don't have to worry about.

I know just about everybody tells you not to feed me table scraps, but I love table scraps. I *love them*, I *really do*! Picture eating

My American Kennel Club name is Boyds Valley Gem, but you can call me Ruby. I have two older brothers, one is a golden retriever just like me, and the other is a 20-pound, 4-year-old taby cat named Jack. He likes to think he runs the show at home, and I'm such a nice little sister, I let him have his way.

—Ruby

dog food for the rest of your life, day in and day out. B*ooooooring*, that's with a capital "B." Have you ever tasted the stuff? The next time you feed me, try some. Go ahead, I dare you. Don't worry, it won't kill you. Look at me, I'm still alive and I've eaten hundreds of pounds of the stuff. After you try some, you'll know firsthand what I have to face day after day when I look into my food bowl. And, I guess what I see in my bowl is the same thing most other dogs see in theirs. In fact, I was shocked to learn that dog owners spend an incredible $9 billion each year on pet food compared to $6 billion for baby food.

What I'm going to say next is somewhat controversial, and I know all the dog food manufacturers in the world are going to hate me for saying it, but please feed me table scraps now and then. What do you think people fed dogs before dog food was invented?

Remember, I'm not asking for a plate of filet mignon, *but now that I think of it, that would be nice.* Instead, the next time you're out having dinner, ask for a doggy bag and bring home the leftovers, *but be sure to remember that the leftovers are for me rather than for your midnight snack!* I'll feel as if I've hit the lottery. I know sometimes I act a little spoiled after receiving treats. I pretend I'm a finicky eater and thumb my nose at my regular dog food, but don't worry about me starving myself; after a while, that dog food will look mighty good. I'm not dumb, just holding out for something better. If it doesn't come along, I *will* eat my plain old dog food.

One caution though, don't ever give me any pieces of chicken, turkey, pork, or fish that contain bones. These bones are highly dangerous for me; they can lodge in my throat or sharp pieces of bone can act like daggers and pierce my stomach wall or intestinal tract. I can die from these injuries!

Also, I know all you chocolate lovers will be shocked, but the rumors are true, chocolate can trigger seizures in me, even kill me. It's the natural chemicals in cocoa that put me in danger. Those chemicals are theophylline, theobromine, and phenylethylamine. The purer the chocolate, the more danger I'm in. A couple of bites of a Milky Way bar won't kill me, but several Godiva chocolates or four to six ounces of Baker's chocolate can mean death for a puppy. So please, keep it away from me.

Since we're on the subject of things I need to stay away from, here are a few more to add to the list.

Death cap mushrooms are super dangerous; that's with a capital "S" and a capital "D." *You may have noticed I like to capitalize words. It's just a "dog" thing. It doesn't worry me. After all, if you think about it, you have a lot of strange habits too.*

Peach, cherry, and other fruit pits are also the pits as far as I'm concerned. If I'm lucky enough not to choke on them, they'll probably give me bad stomach aches. That's bad with a capital "B." *Just kidding.*

For your information, dog food is divided into three groups. At the top is premium, followed by grocery, then mill. The cheaper the price, the more grain there is in the mix. If you read the label, you'll notice the ingredient that makes up the most weight is listed first, others follow in descending order by weight.

Foods high in grain sometimes give me a problem you're probably aware of...it's... it's...I'm *a little embarrassed to say this... bear with me... I'm blushing...it's...it's...it's... farting. There, I said it.* It's not that I don't have manners, it's that sometimes grain-based dog food is improperly processed and it ferments in my intestines. The outcome: gas. *I mean that literally.* If you find I have this problem, try giving me food with a lower grain content—it'll make us both happier.

A new item on the market is gourmet pet food. It's a spin-off of the gourmet dog bakeries that are popping up. The "doggy biscotti," "chicken-flavored bagel," and "peanut-topped ice cream" have especially caught my attention. I'd love to try some, but since I can't drive, I'm hoping you'll pick up some of the new canine cuisine once in a while.

I know it's tough to find the time to grocery shop for me, especially when you barely find the time to shop for yourself. I also know one of the last things you need to worry about as you heat up something for yourself in the microwave is whether I'm eating a well-balanced diet, so here's a simple summary: feed me the best quality dry or canned dog food you can afford, and every once in a while treat me to some leftover meat, rice, bread, cheese, fruit, or vegetables. Go easy on the junkfood. *That goes for you too*!

When it comes to feeding me, there are two ways you can go about it. The choices are "limited portions several times per day" or "continuous access." Guess what I vote for. You're right, continuous access! When first given continuous access—*I prefer to think of it as a doggie buffet*—I might stuff my face for a few days, but after that I'll taper off and only eat as much as my body needs. That's if I don't have company. I hate to admit I get a little greedy if I'm fed with other dogs around. I don't mean to be rude; it's just the "wolf" in me. I instinctively gorge myself because I fear the other dogs will eat everything. This gorging instinct around other dogs sometimes triggers growling, but luckily that growling rarely turns into fighting, because in the dog world there are two unwritten rules that I love. These rules are unbreakable, no three-strikes-before-you're-out rule here. These rules are that the top dog eats first, and food in or near a dog's mouth belongs to it; no other dog, not even a top dog can take it. I *bet you wished that rule existed for parking spaces*.

If I do have a weight problem, and I hate to admit it but many dogs do, it's probably being compounded by lack of exercise. So please take me, your beloved pudgy pooch, for walks more often. Both of us would probably look better and also be a lot healthier. After all, any extra weight on either of us makes our hearts pump harder, our blood pressure go higher, and generally cuts time off our lives.

I'm now going to explain something you've probably always wondered about. No, it's not the meaning of life; it's the answer to the question, "Why do I nibble on grass?" The answer is simple: dogs like veggies too. As I've mentioned earlier, we love meat, but hey, I've noticed you like salad with your steak too. Grass isn't something we crave all the time, but we dogs aren't dumb. We notice all those nice, long, tasty blades, and sometimes a quick snack just makes good dog sense.

Sometimes, however, I purposely eat a lot of grass for another reason. Overindulging on grass triggers me to throw up, which is not necessarily a bad thing, particularly when my stomach is upset.

Since we're talking about my mouth, now is a good time to tell you I realize I sometimes have bad breath; I've heard you call it "dog breath." I want you to know I'm very self-conscious about it, *just like you are when it comes to "morning breath."* You see, many dog food manufacturers add garlic and onion to perk up flavor. As you know, those ingredients can add up to indigestion. In many cases my bad breath stems from that. Sorry.

I do want you to know that dry dog food and treats, such as rawhide chew toys or fresh beef bones from the butcher, exercise my teeth and gums. That exercise helps keep tartar under control. And, while I've eyed your tartar-control toothpaste, something tells me we'll both be happier with the dog bone method.

Every once in a while during my regular vet visits, be sure that the dog doc takes a look at my teeth. The doc will let you know if I need additional tartar control.

• I Love Running Around Naked •

A Look at My Body

I know that a while back humans gave Bo Derek a ten. As for me, I can comfortably say I'm an eight. Go ahead, take a look at my body. It's truly incredible. It's so amazing I'm not even ashamed to run around naked!

The drawing on the next page, which I can proudly say I posed for myself, is pretty self-explanatory, but there are a few interesting things I want to point out. The "withers" is the highest point of my shoulders, behind my neck. This is the spot where my height is measured. My "muzzle" extends to my "stop," which is the area just before or between my eyes. And if you use the word "skull" to describe my whole head, you're technically wrong. The word "skull" describes just the top of it. And just to confuse you a little more, the highest point of my skull is called the "occiput." Hey, I didn't name by body parts, humans did. I also want to let you know that "flews" are long, overhanging upper lips, and my "dewlap" is that loose skin under my neck. And one last thing I want to mention; a bit ago I told you I didn't have feathers, but I neglected to mention I do have "feathering," which is the word humans use to describe the fringes of long fur on my belly, ears, legs, and tail.

My Body Parts

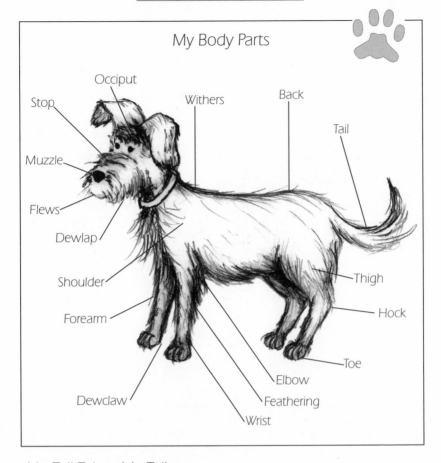

Occiput

Stop

Withers

Back

Tail

Muzzle

Flews

Dewlap

Shoulder

Thigh

Hock

Forearm

Toe

Dewclaw

Elbow

Feathering

Wrist

No Tall Tale—My Tail

I know you're dying to ask me why I have a tail. The answer is "the better to wag with." Just kidding! No one really knows why some animals have tails, not even me, but dog researchers are pretty sure my tail enhances my communication. For you to fully understand this, I have to reveal some fairly personal information. I have two scent-releasing glands just inside my anal area. These sac glands contain at least 12 different substances which carry more information about me than a wallet ever could. When I meet another dog for the first time, my tail is usually upright. That position allows my scent to be smelled at its strongest. The other dog and I will do some serious sniffing. I know this behavior embarrasses you, but please try to understand that it's instinctive, so no matter how loudly you yell at me, it's next to impossible for me to stop doing this.

Individual scents tell us just about everything we need to know about each other. Whether we're male or female, healthy or sick, in heat or not. You get the point.

If I put my tail between my legs when I meet a dog, I may be trying to prevent my odor from being smelled. This usually means I'm lower in the pack than this dog and I'm just being respectful, possibly even a little afraid. As I mentioned earlier, dog manners are different from human manners. If you don't believe me, you can ask Miss Manners.

I also want to let you know that my tail contains scent-marking glands. So now you know another of my little secrets. Whatever my tail brushes against is marked with my odor. Yes, that includes all your stuff too.

Why I wag my tail is also a Perry Mason mystery. Most researchers believe that it's an instinctive behavior, similar to human smiling. Have you ever wondered why you smile? Some researchers say when a human smiles, it's an action stemming from a primitive nervous submission. Picture this! Thousands of years ago that same primitive man who picked up a wolf cub runs into another human in the wild. He unconsciously "smiles" to show he's not posing a threat. So maybe my tail wagging is a combination of friendly anticipation and a little unconscious fear. By the way, we dogs usually don't start wagging our tails until we're about one month old, and then no matter what the age, we never wag our tails when alone. We only wag when we encounter other living things. You see, some humans with a whole lot of extra time on their hands videotaped some of us and uncovered that little secret—no company, no wagging.

While there are puzzles surrounding my tail, I do know if you ever see me chasing my tail, that probably means I'm bored. That's spelled with a capital "B," "O," "R," "E," and "D." Please spend some time with me before I really go stir crazy.

Yes, these are really my ears! They've earned me the nickname Angel Ears, and even I admit they look a little like angel wings! My human dad is a farmer. I keep him company by following him up and down the vineyard rows while he drives his tractor. When we reach the halfway point, I like to sit in the shade under some vines and wait until he comes back across. It's not that I'm lazy, it's just that I'm smart enough to know he's coming back.

—Angel Ears

By the way, "docking" means the amputation of a dog's tail. Thank goodness it's going out of style. It used to be really popular. Many four-day-old puppies had all or part of their tails chopped off just because some humans thought it looked nice.

Pedal Power—My Legs And Paws

As you know, most dogs can't outrun rabbits, but I can beat you to the finish line any day. You have to face the fact that no matter how often you go to the gym, I can outrun you. Most dogs can hit anywhere from 25 to 35 miles per hour while running short distances. Racing greyhounds are the fastest canines around; some can clock in at almost 45 miles per hour.

Dogs were made to run. A peek at my feet proves that—oh, by the way, I prefer to call them paws.

Each paw has four toes. And, I'm not ashamed to admit I'm digitigrade, which means I walk on my toes. You should try it sometime; it's fun! I must admit my toes don't enable me to grasp objects like your fingers can. But boy, can I kick up some dirt when I run.

> **"The next time you discover my teeth marks on something of yours, please try to understand that chewing is one of the few simple pleasures in my life."**

Powerful paws and legs aren't the only physical attributes that make me quick. My shoulder blades aren't directly attached to the rest of my skeleton. This adds up to long strides, which in turn, adds up to speed.

In case you're wondering what those "thumb-looking" things are on the inside of my paws, they're called "dewclaws." They're part of my evolutionary past with no current purpose, just like your appendix. I have dewclaws on each of my forepaws and occasionally on my back legs. My dewclaws don't touch the ground like my toes do.

Since we've been talking about my paws, I guess now is the time to tell you I feel badly when I accidentally scratch you with my claws, which I've noticed you call nails. They grow just like your nails, so to help keep me from hurting you, please have them trimmed by a dog groomer, or if that's too expensive, you can trim my claws yourself every few months with a special clipper made just for canines, or you can even file them with a metal emery board. I promise I'll try to sit still.

The Better To Bite (Bones) With—My Teeth

Adult humans have 32 permanent teeth; I have ten more. Feel free to count mine if you don't believe me, but better be careful, I might bite. Just kidding again!

When you have a puppy in the house, you'll probably find baby teeth lying around. Don't freak out. Puppies lose all of their 28 baby teeth just like you lost all 20 of your baby teeth.

When I'm about four months old, my permanent teeth start to come in and my desire to chew on things skyrockets. Please stop yelling at me long enough to try to understand that I'm just trying to ease the pain. Actually, I'd really appreciate it if you'd occasionally rub ice cubes on my gums while I'm teething. Just like for human babies, ice numbs my gums. The numbness eases the pain, which in turn lessens my desire to sink my teeth into that messy pile of clothing and shoes you have on the floor of your closet. *Didn't think I knew that pile of stuff was there, did you?*

By the time I'm about six months old, the tooth fairy is through visiting, but I must confess, I usually don't give up my love for chewing. So the next time you discover my teeth marks on something of yours, please try to understand that chewing is one of the few simple pleasures in my life. Please respect these little pleasures by providing me with my own things to chew. They don't have to be expensive, a large knuckle bone from the meat department will do, just as well as a big knot of old rope. However, don't give me an old shoe, because I won't be able to tell the difference between one of your new shoes and "my" old shoe.

By the way, the four vampire-looking teeth in my mouth are

called canines, just like the word used to describe dogs. You have four cuspids that look like fangs too, and sometimes I've heard you call them your canine teeth. I consider that a compliment. I also have twelve incisors, sixteen premolars, and ten molars. Those teeth are set into powerful jaws. Most dogs can easily bite through a human limb. Aren't you glad we choose not to?

Where's The Blow Dryer?—My Fur

My hair, referred to as fur, grows in cycles. That's the reason for my "bad hair days," what's yours? *Just kidding. I love your hair, even in the morning when it's sticking up all over the place. You probably didn't think I notice these things, but I do.* I usually experience two major shedding and growth periods each year, one in the spring, the other in the fall. These cycles are triggered by the amount of sunlight in a day, which is called the photo period. *Boy, that dictionary sure is coming in handy.* By the way, poodles are just some of the few dogs that break this rule; they don't shed much at all no matter what time of year it is. And to tell you the truth, I don't always follow the rule myself when you keep me in the house year-round. That's because artificial light throws off my system and I shed all the time. Now wait a minute, I'm not complaining about being in the house—*I loooooove being inside*—it's just that I feel badly when my fur covers the sofa, the floor, and just about everything else in the house. You know, I'd help clean up if I could. I've always dreamed of running the vacuum cleaner. Actually, I have a thing about vacuum cleaners, but I'll tell you more about that later.

I notice you wash your hair every day, but there's no need to wash my fur that often. Every time you bathe me, you're washing away the natural oils in my skin. Without these oils, my skin becomes dry and irritated. As a general rule, brush me often and only bathe me when I'm dirty. If I'm an "inside" dog, bathe me no more than twice a month. If I'm an "outside" dog, twice a year is fine as far as I'm concerned.

I know bathing me isn't on your top-ten list of ways to spend a pleasant afternoon. Sometimes, it looks as if you're the one being bathed, not me, and I know how badly wet dog fur smells. Remember my sense of smell is sharper than yours.

So when it comes to the business of baths, here are two helpful hints that will make things go smoother: First, be firm with me. Second, use warm, not cold, water. If you're tempted to just turn on the outside hose and not deal with filling a tub with heated H_2O, it's only natural that I'll squirm. Before you lose patience with me, please remember the last time you stepped into your shower and found the water temperature wasn't as warm as you thought. Actually, it must have been downright freezing. I heard you yelling, and I'm not one hundred percent positive, but I think I also heard you cussing. *Don't worry, I won't repeat what you said.*

Now, where was I—oh, yeah, soaking my fur will require some elbow grease, and that's because it has a water-resistant quality that comes in handy when it rains—*Mother Nature's version of a dog umbrella*, I guess.

Please use pet shampoo on me, not human shampoo or dishwashing liquid; after all, I'm not a person or a plate. Also, please be careful not to get the shampoo in my eyes. Just like yours, my eyes will sting. Don't forget to wash the inside of my ear flaps, and please try to leave the lather on my fur for several minutes so the flea-and-tick medication can do its job. Then rinse my fur well. When it comes to drying me off, let me pretend I'm Elvis. I *looooove trying to shake all that water off me. Feels soooooo good*!

Dry bath products can also do the trick. The next time you're at the pet store, look these over.

Here's another option: self-service dog washing salons. These businesses supply the tubs, hoses, and water. You supply the man power. I like to think of them as doggie car washes, but luckily dogs are dried with towels and blow dryers, not those long, hard flaps. I've noticed these self-service businesses are popping up just about everywhere. If there's one in our town, let's check it out.

If cost isn't a concern, forget self-service and head to full service. That means you drop me off at the dog groomer's, and when you pick me up, I'll look wonderful and I'll smell pretty good too. The groomer does all the work. Simpler, but more expensive.

As you've probably noticed, fur fluffiness varies from breed to breed. Most dogs have a layer of super-soft fur covered with coarser fur. Did you know a husky's inner layer of fur is as warm as goose down? That's why a husky doesn't shiver in subfreezing temperatures. However, most breeds aren't as well insulated. So please, let me in the house on chilly days *and that way I won't become a chili dog*! I'd appreciate it. As I age, consider outfitting me in a sweater for added warmth. Years and years of socialization have lessened my toughness when it comes to the elements. *By the way, the color of the sweater doesn't matter, but if you really want to know, I've always wanted a sweater with cute little kitties on it.*

You probably think there are only three uses for my fur: keeping me warm, messing up your clothes, and making your friends sneeze. But there are more. Try sprinkling some of my fur in your garden. It's guaranteed to keep away rabbits and squirrels. I think the smell of my fur is what does the trick. If you don't have a problem with rabbits and squirrels, no need to sprinkle.

By the way, birds love my fur; they consider it a special prize. When they spot it, they risk life and limb to swoop down and grab it. They use it to help build their nests. *I wonder if this puts me in the construction business? You know, a construction equipment supplier? I wonder if I can get in trouble with the* IRS. *I'll have to think about this.*

While checking out my nose you may have noticed my long whiskers. They're officially called vibrissae. These thick strands of hair also appear on my legs and other areas of my body. If you're tempted to trim them, please don't; you see, they're supersensitive to touch. They help me figure out if a space is too tight to get through and in general enhance my sense of touch. *Think of them as my "feelers," furry feelers, that is.*

• *We're a Family!* •

Background, Breeds & Instincts

F riends might have told you I'm an animal that loves being part of a pack. I hate to break the news to you, but it's true. Here's something else that may shock you—you're a "pack animal" too. Maybe that's why we get along so well.

Just like a human being, I love being part of a group. Have you noticed that every time we go for a walk, people and animals always catch my attention? But don't get jealous; I'm still content if our "group" is made up of just you and me.

Most scientists agree that the branches of my family tree lead back to wolves. I hate to brag, but I was one of the first wild animals which ALLOWED itself to be tamed. This happened between 12,000 and 14,000 years ago. My first job: hunting companion.

Wolves travel in packs to survive. In order to keep things running smoothly, there's always a head honcho. The alpha wolf is always the biggest, the strongest, the one that leads the hunt for food, the one that sets the rules. Does that sound like you? Sure does to me.

You see, as far as I'm concerned, you're the head dog in our family. Now, wait a minute, don't get offended because I'm calling you a dog. I'm a dog; some of my best friends are dogs and my brothers and sisters are dogs. Sure, you look different. You're not covered with fur, but hey, that's OK, because I don't judge people by their looks.

As far as I'm concerned, you and your family are a dog pack which has welcomed me into your den with open paws—oops, I mean arms.

"Imprinting" enables me to have such an open mind. Let me explain; normally, while I'm between the ages of four to twelve weeks old, whatever animal I spend most of my time with I'll consider part of my family. *That explains those pictures of confused canines that think rabbits, cats, or turtles are their moms.* Luckily, most puppies are exposed to the human animal during this critical period of socialization.

Blue Blood

As I mentioned, my great, great, great, great, great, great, great, great, great grandfather was a wolf. Today, there are about 400 breeds of dogs. Some of us still look like wolves, but most of us don't. Breeding is the reason, and humans have played a big part in that.

Humans gained genetic control over us through selective breeding. *Boy, when I phrase it like that, it sounds awful. Let me try again.* When dogs were first domesticated, we all looked pretty much the same. Then humans stepped in. They'd pick a quality they wanted to emphasize, then they'd breed a particular dog that possessed that quality with another that shared the quality.

So now there are giant Irish wolfhounds that weight in at more than 200 pounds and tiny Chihuahuas and Yorkshire terriers that you could carry in your pockets if you wanted to, *but I don't know why you would; I wouldn't want to carry around a human.* Anyway, back to what I was talking about, which was that selective breeding has also led to miniaturization and dwarfism. There is a difference between these two genetically created conditions. Dogs that have been miniaturized—I *prefer to think of them as being shrunk*—are smaller all over. Dogs that have been made into dwarfs keep the same body size, just their legs are shortened.

Selective breeding has also created dogs that love to swim and some who can't even stand walking on wet grass, *like the dog I met at the park the other day*! Golden retrievers, Labradors, spaniels, and poodles are just some of the dogs that especially love the water. The Portuguese water dog is another canine that is so comfortable in H_2O that years ago this breed was actually used to herd fish. *If I didn't know better, I would think all these dogs, along with the Newfoundland, with its funny-looking webbed feet and funnier looking rudder-like tail, are sea otters masquerading as dogs.*

> **"Classifying us dogs is not an exact science; it's arbitrary."**

While I just told you the Newfoundland is a great swimmer, I have to admit it's not one of the best watchdogs around, *probably wouldn't even make much of a lifeguard*. Rottweilers and German shepherds were bred especially as watchdogs. And, you may not believe this, but it's true: Chihuahuas make pretty good watchdogs too. *They are truly little dogs with big attitudes.*

Classifying us dogs is not an exact science; it's arbitrary. It changes from year to year, country to country, dog expert to dog expert, but for the most part, breeds of dogs fall into seven categories: hounds, sporting dogs, herding dogs, terriers, working dogs, nonsporting dogs, and toys.

It's important that you know these categories, because when you're selecting a dog to share your life with, you have to realize that while each one of us is unique, genetics, triggered by selective breeding, plays a big part in determining our nature, and in turn, our behavior.

Think of it this way, you often store your ID in your wallet, which I've seen you stuff into the pocket of your jeans. Well, I keep my identification in my genes too. *The difference is, my genes aren't Levis or Calvin Kleins.*

Hounds

If I were a gambler, *which luckily I'm not*...OK, OK, I *admit, I'd love to scratch a lottery ticket if I could*...I'd bet the hound is the oldest breed of dog around. Throughout history, hounds have been by man's side, helping him to hunt. As a matter of fact, before the development of the gun, their presence was crucial; they often made the difference between a successful hunt and hungry people around the campfire.

There are two types of hounds: scent hounds and sight hounds. Sight hounds were originally bred to spot prey from a distance, silently chase it, then kill it. That's why they're long, lean, tall muscle machines that usually don't bark while they run. Also, their eyesight is the best in the canine kingdom.

Scent hounds were bred to steadily make their way toward prey by following odor trails. The noses of scent hounds, especially bloodhounds, are impressive, to say the least. Actually, humans can't even begin to comprehend how well the noses of scent hounds work, *even I have trouble, and my nose works really well.* Scent hounds usually have short, sturdy legs and long ears. Their legs enable them to put that little pink Eveready Energizer bunny to shame, because scent hounds can go for hours and hours and hours when hot on a trail, dare I say *doggedly* pursuing the quarry. Their short legs keep their noses close to the ground. Their long ears also help them while they're tracking: the flaps act like fans, blowing the scents into their faces. Even the lips of scent hounds get into the act. Moisture on them traps scent particles. As I mentioned earlier, sight hounds work quietly, but scent hounds like to whistle while they work, so to speak, but just between you and me, what comes out of their mouths sounds more like barking.

History is full of hunting hounds. 5,000 years ago sight hounds outran desert gazelles. In the Middle Ages, French kings had huge packs of scent hounds, with some packs numbering up to one thousand dogs. Many of these scent hounds received royal treatment, and it was common for favorites to live in the palaces.

If I were a hound, my ideal human companion would be an avid hunter who'd use my tracking abilities, but I'd also thrive in a household run by people who love the outdoors. We'd hunt, fish, hike, and camp together. I'd also enjoy living with families that have kids and big backyards. After all, hounds love and need to be active. One of their biggest pluses is that they're very comfortable around humans. Hounds were bred for that. But as hounds would be the first to admit, they're not the best listeners around. Sometimes they'll choose to ignore your commands while they're following their sense of smell or sight. It's not that hounds don't want to do what you say, it's just that their instincts are so strong; sometimes instinct gets the better of them.

> ## Types of hounds include:
>
> *Sight hounds*
> Afghan, borzoi, deerhound, greyhound, Irish wolfhound, saluki, whippet
>
> *Scent hounds*
> basset hound, beagle, bloodhound, dachshund, English foxhound, harrier, otterhound

Sporting Dogs

Once man began carrying guns, so-called sporting dogs, which are also known as gundogs, were bred by crossing hounds with herding dogs. Their purpose was to retrieve game shot by hunters. Sporting dogs are usually divided into five groups: setters, pointers, retrievers, flushing, and water dogs.

Setters were taught by hunters to crouch or "sit," facing in the direction where they sensed game. Pointers also freeze when they spot game; then they use their forelegs to point toward the prey. When I first heard about this, I thought, wow, man must be pretty smart to have thought of this hunting technique and these dogs must be even smarter to be able to learn this trick, but then I found out wolves do something similar. After alerting the rest of the hunting pack to the location of prey, a wolf will lie hidden, waiting for his buddies to drive the prey in his direction.

Retrievers don't sit; they move. They recover game that has been wounded or killed by carrying it gently in their mouths, and no matter how hungry they are, they won't take a bite, *even a teeny-weeny one.* This breed was initially bred to retrieve waterfowl and

Types of sporting dogs include:

setters
Brittany, English setter, French spaniel, Gordon setter, Irish red-and-white setter, Irish setter, Picardy setter

pointers
Bracco Italiana, Czeksy Fousek, English pointer, German shorthaired pointer, German wirehaired pointer, Portuguese pointer, Spanish pointer

retrievers
flat-coated retriever, golden retriever, Hungarian vizsla, Kooikerhondje, Labrador retriever, Nova Scotia duck tolling retriever

flushing dogs
American cocker spaniel, clumber spaniel, English cocker spaniel, English springer spaniel, field spaniel, Sussex spaniel, Welsh springer spaniel

water dogs
barbet, German corded poodle, Hungarian puli, Irish water spaniel, Portuguese water dog, Spanish water dog, standard poodle

fish, but nowadays it can serve just about any type of hunter. What I'm going to say next may surprise you, but it's true. Years ago, after a long day of work, many retrievers caught their own fish for dinner. *Wow, wouldn't that have been neat to see: a dog out fishing.*

Wolves retrieve also, and for all I know, they probably fish too! Retrieving wolves bring food to nursing she-wolves and wolf cubs so they won't starve.

Last I heard, flushing dogs are banning together to try and educate people on the background of their name. They've told me they're tired of people thinking of toilets whenever their category is mentioned. They want people to know they're called flushing dogs because they "flush" out prey for hunters from heavily vegetated areas.

On the other hand, water dogs couldn't be happier with their name. They consider H_2O part of their address.

If I were a sporting breed, I'd make an ideal family pet. That's because sporting dogs are more trainable than most other dogs. They're bred to do exactly what you tell them to do, especially Labrador retrievers, which by the way, are the most popular breed of dog in the United States. *In case you're wondering, golden retrievers are the second most popular and German shepherds are third.*

Herding Dogs

Humans like to say that herding dogs are the most intelligent of all dogs. But, as I pointed out earlier, these guys are just doing what they were bred to do.

The behavior of herding dogs was established thousands of years ago when nomadic shepherds in Asia bred dogs to protect and control their herds. Today, herding dogs handle just about any animal you can imagine. They're even used to scare geese and ducks from airports and golf courses.

One of the most famous of the herding breeds is the Border collie. It comes from the reindeer–herding dogs brought to Scotland by Viking invaders. If you've never seen a Border collie at work, you're really missing something. I *can watch one for hours*. Sheep dogs are also pretty cool to watch. I've heard the true sign of a good sheep dog or Border collie is when the animals it's herding respect it, rather than fear it.

Just like tracking, setting, and retrieving, this herding ability comes from wolves. While hunting for food, wolves often encircle their prey, then direct its movement.

Herding dogs can work in groups or alone. But let me tell you, a herding dog working alone has its job cut out for it. When it realizes that other members of its herding pack aren't in place, it rushes about doing all their jobs. Its instinct demands this.

If you choose a herding dog as a pet, remember it needs a lot, and I do mean a lot, of physical and mental exercise. If I were a herding dog, I could only be truly happy if I had plenty of outdoor activity.

> ## Types of herding dogs include:
>
> Australian cattle dog, Australian shepherd, bearded collie, Border collie, German shepherd, Old English sheepdog, Shetland sheepdog

Terriers

When most humans see an Australian silky or a Yorkshire they think, "Oh, how cute. I have to have one!" They think these dogs are terriers, but they're wrong; in my opinion, they're terrorists. OK, OK, OK, *I take that back, but you have to agree, terriers are feisty and that's definitely spelled with a capital "F."* These small hunting dogs were originally bred to kill vermin, such as rats, and dig out small mammals from their dens. *"Terra" means earth in Latin, get it?* Terriers have short legs and sharp teeth, perfect for tracking

> ## Types of terriers include:
>
> Airedale terrier, Australian silky terrier, Border terrier, Irish terrier, Kerry blue terrier, miniature schnauzer, Scottish terrier

down such animals as rats, foxes, badgers, and weasels. And, just for your information, after a terrier tracks one of these animals, get ready to see a fight, because a terrier won't back down.

I've probably scared you. You're now probably thinking a terrier is the last type of dog you want to bring home, but surprise, surprise, surprise, terriers make great pets. They're fun to be around. At all the dog gatherings I've been to, they're the life of the party. They have a mind of their own and are full of energy and are always entertaining. They make pretty good watchdogs too, and city life doesn't bother them at all. They like all the hustle and bustle. And, here's something for you to think about: terriers usually survive serious illness better than most other dogs. Maybe it's something in their strong personalities.

> Types of working dogs include:
>
> Akita, boxer, Doberman pinscher, Great Dane, Rottweiler, Saint Bernard, Siberian husky

Working Dogs

This class of dog was bred to make man's working life easier. In the past, working dogs did everything from pulling carts loaded to the brim with heavy items to turning waterwheels, butter churns, even roasting turnspits. I'm not kidding, dogs were placed in circular treadmills, called turnspits, right next to huge cooking fires. The treadmills were connected to roasting spits and as the dogs walked in circles, meat on the spits was rotated and roasted. *Thank goodness ovens and microwaves are the way to go nowadays.*

The dizzy dogs that spent their lives going around and around on treadmills were bred for long bodies, short legs, and endurance. Dogs that pulled carts were bred for strength. Many of these breeds had rough lives. At the end of the day, they truly were dog-tired. As a matter of fact, abuse of working dogs played a big part in the formation of the American Society for the Prevention of Cruelty to Animals in 1866.

If I were one of these working dogs and you were going to take me home, I'd want you to remember that I will need lots and lots of physical exercise, but I will also be very self-sufficient.

Nonsporting Dogs

Nonsporting dogs are breeds that were bred for unique purposes. For instance, dalmatians were bred as guard dogs for the riding coaches of royalty. *No wonder they enjoyed being the stars of that Disney movie.* Here's something you may not know about dalmatians: they're born pure white and only later develop spots. Lhasa apso were bred to sound the alarm at the Dalai Lama's palace and chow chows were bred as a food supply—luckily, that use has gone out of style, but the name is still in fashion!

> ### Types of nonsporting dogs include:
> Boston terrier, bulldog, chow chow, dalmatian, Finnish spitz, keeshound, Lhasa apso

Hey, have you ever wondered why English bulldogs look like they do? Well, they were bred for huge jaws and short noses. The reason for this genetic manipulation was to enable these dogs to most effectively help hunters bring down wild bulls. Bulldogs were trained to attack, then hang on for their dear lives. Their short noses allowed them to breathe while their faces were smashed against bulls. *Boy, what a life.* And, to top things off, most bulldogs have such big heads they actually have to be delivered by cesarean section.

If I were a nonsporting dog, and you were thinking of taking me home, here's something important I would really want you to know: odds are I have inborn health problems or the potential for health problems. The health issues of nonsporting dogs stem from humans having taken various physical traits to an extreme by selective breeding. For instance, English bulldogs have so many breathing, heart, jaw, and teeth problems that their life expectancy is 20 percent less than that of other dogs. Please don't let these health issues scare you off. After all, they weren't caused by those nice nonsporting dogs themselves; humans created them. I'm not trying to make you feel badly, I'm just being honest.

Toys

If you want a dog that truly loves to be spoiled, get a dog from the toy group. They weren't bred to hunt or herd; actually, they weren't bred to do anything but be

> Types of toys include:
> Chihuahua, Maltese, Pekingese, Pomeranian, pug, toy poodle, Shih Tzu

cute companions for humans. These dogs are usually pretty small. I was thumbing through the *Golden Book Encyclopedia* and read that the ancient Greeks loved to breed tiny lapdogs. These dogs were meant to be held in a lady's lap. The purpose was to keep her tummy warm. *I guess with no central heating, they had to think of something, so they created hot dogs.*

If I were a toy dog, and you were considering me as a pet, I'd ask for only two things: first, that you keep me close, because I was bred with the desire for human companionship. Second, that you remember I'm really not a toy; I'm a dog with ancestors that were wolves. Please respect that.

I jokingly call these seven categories *The Magnificent Seven*, and that's because, while I liked the movie, it's not being shown in any theaters now. It's a thing of the past, just like these categories are becoming. Nowadays, most dogs aren't bred for speed and tracking ability; they're bred for submissiveness and friendliness. That's OK, because it brings me to another canine group, one which I believe will finally start getting the respect it deserves: random-bred dogs. The dogs in this category are known by a number of names: mutts, mixed, mongrels. These labels don't upset me. I know firsthand that most random-bred dogs are the hardiest, healthiest, and most heartwarming pets around.

• Old Habits Are Hard to Break •

Understanding Why I Do What I Do

OK, OK, OK, I know I have some annoying habits, but, hey, so do you. I guess at the top of your list of "things that I do that drive you up the wall" is my habit of, well, ah, how can I best put this? I guess I'll just come right out and say it, my habit of peeing on everything I possibly can. Hey, I'm just marking my territory. It's a natural thing. When you're settling into a new job, or classroom, don't you determine which desk is yours and then proceed to put your own stuff all over it—sort of to mark it as yours? Well, this is a similar situation; I *just don't happen to own any pens and pencils*. So please remember when I'm marking things, my action means much more than just relieving myself. It's an instinctual thing for me.

Since we're talking about "peeing," *oh, come on, say it, it's not that bad a word, actually, it's kind of fun to say. Here we go..."peeing." See, I told you it's fun to say.* Did you know all puppies squat when taking care of business? When a male dog is eight or nine months old, it begins to cock its leg. Some female dogs do this too; it's rare, but true. Admit it, don't be embarrassed, you've seen me. I've noticed a puzzled look on your face when I cock my leg as high as I can.

Despite my appearance, I'm not trying to do the splits; I'm just trying to leave my scent at nose level. Some dog researchers even speculate that I'm trying to give the next dog that comes along the impression that I'm taller and bigger than I really am. *Maybe I am, maybe I'm not. I think I'll keep this little secret to myself.*

Since we're on the subject of relieving myself, here are several more things I'd like to share with you.

You've probably heard I don't soil where I sleep. Well, that's usually true. But it's not instinctive; it's a learned behavior. You see, when I'm born I can't go to the bathroom on my own. My mom has to lick parts of my body in order to kick-start my bowels. I know this next bit of information will gross you out, but it's common for her to swallow what I eliminate. This goes on for several weeks, then out of the blue, she begins to get upset with me when I soil our den. I must admit, I'm confused because as far as I'm concerned, last week it was OK to go to the bathroom in my bed and now I'm being made to feel as if I've committed the crime of the century. Her constant nagging gets on my nerves, but it does do the trick. Before I know it, I'm leaving the den when I need to take care of business.

By the way, wolves don't soil their dens either. They don't want odor from their waste to give away their location. It could cost them their lives!

If you need to house-train me, begin by controlling my food and water intake, then monitor how often I "go" after waking, eating, drinking, and playing. Then do what humans love to do—step in and take control. Consistently show me where you want me to take care of business. You may even want to repeat a key word as I go to the bathroom. I'll soon associate that word with relieving myself.

Sounds confusing? Relax, just think of it this way, as a toddler you were taken to the bathroom when you needed to go. Now as an adult, no matter where you are, if you have to go, you automatically think, "I have to go to the bathroom," and that's where you head. Please be patient with me like your parents were with you while you learned. Also remember, just like you, I prefer praise. If you praise me, instead of yell at me, I'll learn a lot quicker.

If I do have an accident in the house, don't rub my nose in it; that doesn't help, it only gets my nose dirty. You may want to treat the area with an odor neutralizer. You can pick some up at any pet store. You see, home cleaners usually won't get rid of the smell and the next time I need to go, odor from that area will draw me to it. Just like a magnet, *a smelly one.*

I've noticed most of the time you look away when I'm taking care of business. I appreciate the privacy, but every now and then take a peek at my poop. Small, firm stools are proof that my digestive system is on track. An added bonus to my having small, firm stools is that cleanup is easier.

My stool may be soft for a variety of reasons, and a common one may be that I'm eating food that is poor in nutrients. A hard stool may indicate a mineral or fiber imbalance in my diet. For instance, too many bones from the butcher's will result in white, rock-hard stools. I *know that for a fact, because* I *learned the hard way.*

Remember those anal scent sacs I told you about? Well, I use them to sprinkle more scent on my stool just before I eliminate it from my system. As I said, scent is very important to me.

If you see me dragging by rear end on the ground, I'm not asking for toilet paper. Those scent sacs in my anal area are probably clogged and sore, and I'm just trying to get some relief. My problem should clear up in a few days, but if it doesn't, our vet can drain the sacs; it's a simple procedure, but a little on the gross side.

One last thing, sometimes after taking care of business, I claw at the ground around my stool. No human knows for sure why I do this, and to tell you the truth, I've been doing it for so long, I've forgotten what triggered the habit, but I do have sweat glands between by toes and I might be adding more of my scent to the area, and you know my scent is my calling card.

Watch Me, I Can Kiss Your Face—How to Stop Me from Jumping on You

Probably second on your list of my annoying habits is when I jump on you. I'm just trying to reach your face so I can show you some affection by licking it. It's a habit I picked up as a puppy; I used to love to lick my mom's face. If I were lucky, she'd regurgitate a small amount of food for me, just like wolves do for their cubs. Don't worry, I don't expect you to throw up. To tell you the truth, it would shock me if you did, because as I mature, "licking" in my world becomes similar to "kissing" in your world. *It's not my fault you insist on standing on two feet, which makes you taller than me!*

I know you hate it when I jump on you. I sometimes scratch you and often mess up your clothes. I think panty hose manufacturers should give every dog a huge bag of biscuits... yearly. That's

> **❝I think panty hose manufacturers should give every dog a huge bag of biscuits ...yearly.❞**

because I bet dogs are responsible for the purchase of more nylons than all the advertising campaigns combined.

Where was I? I got sidetracked just thinking about all those dog biscuits. Oh yeah, there are several things you can do to get me to stop jumping on you. Here are three of the easiest. First, gently step on my hind toes while I have my front paws on you. If that doesn't work, try grabbing my front paws and pushing me backward. If I still don't get the message, knee me in the chest, *gently.* All three tactics send the same message, and that message is, every time I jump on you, it hurts. I don't like pain, so after awhile, I'll put two and two together. Praise is also a great motivator, so when you can tell I want to jump on you, but I don't, let me know I've pleased you.

This is the fence that separates us from the flower garden in our yard. Boy, would we just love to get in there and sniff the flowers. We wonder why our owner doesn't open the gate and let us play in her flower bed.
—Mug and Moose

Woof, Woof, Woof—How to Stop Me from Barking

I know your neighbors are upset about my barking, and sometimes you lose your patience with me when it's 3:00 in the morning and I'm being "vocal." But, hey again, it's your fault; humans bred me for the behavior, *and admit it, you don't want me to greet everyone with my tail wagging.* Well, we all know the blame game is counterproductive. So, let's try to figure out some ways to shut me up in certain situations.

The key to solving the problem is to figure out what gets me going. Am I confused? Do you allow me in the house during the day, then at night kick me out? As I mentioned earlier, I'm a pack animal, I need social contact and I don't like being alone. So, my feelings are really hurt when you open the door and order me out. *Let me tell you, it's lonely in the dark with nothing to do but rack my brain trying to figure out what I did wrong.* Try putting my bed outside your bedroom window or sliding glass door. It will work wonders for me just knowing I'm close to you.

Do I bark because my hobby is "fence running?" A lot of dogs excel at this "sport." In my opinion, it should be an Olympic event. I guess I'm getting off track. *Wow, another pun and I wasn't even trying!*

You'll know a fence runner as soon as you see one—it's the dog barking up a storm while racing from one end of a fence to the other end whenever a person or animal is on the other side.

I have to admit fence running is a whole lot of fun and adds excitement to an otherwise boring day, but I know it can get on both your own and your neighbors' nerves. To help break me of this habit, plant some big bushes along the fence, landscape with rocks, or better yet, put me inside during peak sidewalk travel time. That should help address the problem.

I admit I have a tendency to bark when I'm bored. Give me a bone to chew. I'll be so busy munching away, I won't have time to bark as much. Also, the more exercise I get, the less energy I have to get rid of, so don't forget our walks together.

A so-called "throw can" also does wonders when it comes to breaking bad habits such as excessive barking. You can easily make one; just fill an empty can with a few pennies or small stones. Despite the name, don't throw the can at me, just shake it at me when I'm doing something wrong. The noise will startle me and I'll stop what I'm doing. After awhile, just the sight of the can will stop me in my tracks. I recommend you use a soda can, not a beer can. Who knows what your neighbors might think if you start waving a beer can every time I'm barking.

You may also try an old-fashioned approach—just order me to be quiet. As I've told you, I hate it when you're upset with me, so if barking less is the price I have to pay to put a smile on your face, I'm willing to cut back. *The only thing that worries me is your neighbors might prefer my barking over your yelling or the rattle of that throw can!*

Drastic measures can be taken to address excessive barking and fence running. But, as I said, they are drastic and the very idea of these measures makes me shiver, so please think long and hard before resorting to them.

For fence running, you can try a so-called "invisible fence." It works electronically. You bury an antenna wire in our yard. It's hooked to a radio transmitter in our house, which is tied to a tiny computer in my collar. I'll receive an electric shock if I get too close to the invisible fence. After two or three of those shocks, I'll remember what's off limits. Shock collars hurt and that's with a capital "H."

Debarking is the surgical altering of my vocal cords. That's a nice way of saying most of my vocal cords are cut and removed. The procedure leaves me sounding as if I'm getting over a bad case of laryngitis.

And here's just a tidbit to think about the next time I'm barking up a storm and you're wishing I'd shut up. My bark, just like every other dog's, is unique. While you can't tell the difference, dogs can. So please remember, my ability to bark is just as amazing and as precious as your ability to speak.

Chomping Down—How to Stop Me from Chewing

As you know, I love to chew. It's sheer heaven to sink my teeth into shoes, furniture, rolled up newspapers, the corners of walls, broom handles, you name it. *It feels sooooo good!* As I mentioned earlier, I discovered the joy of chewing as a teething puppy. Supplying me with chew toys goes a long way in protecting your possessions. Better yet, a bone from the butcher really hits the spot when it comes to satisfying my craving to chew. *Nothing personal, but I'd take a bone over your new shoes any day.*

Another way to prevent teeth marks on your items is to coat them with bad tasting anti-chew products sold at pet stores. A bad-tasting bite will leave an awful taste in my mouth and that should convince me not to sink my teeth into that item again.

You may think I chew your things to get back at you. You probably think I'm upset because you leave me home alone. Feel guilty if you want, but that's not the case. If you don't believe me, look it up. Research shows I don't act out of spite. Sure, I get stressed when you leave me alone. The first half hour is the worst—I think the latest term for it is "separation anxiety." But I never act out of spite, anxiety yes, boredom yes, spite no. I do have a confession to make. I love it when you feel guilty. I notice the more guilty you feel, the more attention and treats I get when you return home. So, as far as I'm concerned, your guilt is a good thing—needless for you to feel, but usually a very good thing for me.

Trespassing On Our Sofa—How to Keep Me Off the Furniture

I love taking naps on your sofa. I *like to think of it as "our" sofa.* As I've told you, I'm no birdbrain, so who wouldn't prefer a nice,

I know I stand close to the ground, but like the man says, "Your legs only have to be long enough to reach the floor." I know bigger dogs like to chase squirrels and cats and even bigger game, but I like to chase bees and wasps. So far the score is 3-zip and I'm winning!

—Cody

soft spot to a cold, hard floor. But if you're tired of brushing dog fur from your clothes after sitting down, here's a little tip on how to get me to stop. I'm not talking full-scale guerrilla warfare here, but set a trap. Before you go to bed, place a mousetrap on the sofa, and when I think you're asleep and it's safe for me to get comfortable, I'll be in for a big surprise. Do this several times and I'll stay away from *"our"* sofa for sure. This may sound brutal, but don't worry, my movement will set off the mouse trap before I can be hurt.

Pretty Please—How to Stop Me from Begging for Food

I know you hate it when I beg at the table. The best way to stop this is when I'm a puppy, never, never, never feed me food from the table while you're eating. I don't want to grow up into an ill-mannered dog that makes a scene at every meal by begging for food. Just place my food in my bowl before you sit down to eat or feed me after you're done. My brain, trained by routine, enables me to accept this. I may drool a bit, but I will wait my turn.

Stranger Than Strange—How to Stop Me from Eating Feces

Now I admit, this next habit annoys even me, and yet I do it. It's official name is coprophagia. Believe me, it has nothing to do with the fear of cops. I *wish it did*. It's a nice word that describes something gross. It's when I eat stool and I'm not talking about a stool that you sit on. I really don't know why I do this, since I'm not starving. I do know wolves sometimes eat stool for nutrients. I do know that cat "caca" is very high in undigested protein, so maybe that's why some dogs like to nibble.

Some animal experts suspect a dietary deficiency may be to blame for coprophagia. I know humans sometimes crave strange things, even dirt, a condition officially called pica, "the abnormal desire to eat substances not normally eaten." Whatever the case, the less stool around, the less I'm tempted. So, in addition to cleaning up more often, *which* I *do appreciate*, you may want to give my diet a little more thought. Also, don't hesitate to reach for that "throw can."

I'm Confused—How to Help Me Accept Your Marriage and Kids

As I confessed earlier, the wolf in me triggers an obsession with rank. This obsession could cause some problems when you tie the knot. You see, before the wedding, things are pretty clear; you're the coach and I'm the star player. When the love of your life enters the game, all fingers point me to the bench. I'm not trying to be difficult, but my pack logic tells me that's where the "new" player belongs, not me. Now, I know the love of your life won't be too happy about sitting on the bench. So, just explain the situation to me in a firm, not mean, tone of voice. You may even want to let your honey order me around for awhile. I don't mind. You see, I don't have a problem with moving down the pecking order. I just don't like uncertainty. I thrive on predictability. It's this security thing. *Codependency, you know what I mean.*

Just to prepare you, things might again get a little hairy, *or should* I *say furry,* when the two of you have a baby. First, I'm bigger than the baby. Second, the baby constantly does two things that have "submission" stamped all over them. The child rolls on its back and also pees in my presence. When a dog does these things, it's shouting, "Hey, you're the boss." So, these signs and the baby's size tell me the little newcomer should be lower than I am in the pecking order. To set me straight, let me smell the baby's blanket; this will get me used to the little cutie's unique smell. Then in a firm voice constantly remind me that this little bundle of joy is my boss, even if I outweigh the pip-squeak. I may act like a jealous, older, four-legged sibling for a while, but I'll catch on eventually.

• *Puppy Power* •

My Early Years

J ust like a human baby's early years, my first few weeks of life are critical to my development. I'm learning from everything I do. As I wrestle with my brothers and sisters, I'm learning about my strength; when my parents growl at me, I'm learning respect for rank; when I chase balls, I'm learning how to stalk prey.

It's important that I be exposed to humans as a pup, especially beginning the sixth week of my life. If not, I'll be hard to train. This is why a lot of puppies bred for mass sales have so many problems. Not only are some not exposed to humans during this critical socialization period, they don't have much contact with their canine families because many are kept cooped up in cages after being weaned. Sad, but true. Luckily, this type of breeding is going out of style, because large and small pet stores alike are teaming with local animal shelters to find homes for dogs that have been left there instead of buying from mass breeders. Yea!!!

Please make sure I'm at least eight weeks old before you actually bring me home. Before that, I'm not physically and mentally ready for the big move. You see, I still need the security and com-

I kind of think that if the Seven Dwarfs had owned a dog, I'd be it.
—Amanda

panionship of my family. By the way, my siblings are officially called "littermates," *not to be mistaken for "litter bugs" even though they can sure make a mess.*

Bringing me home is less traumatic than bringing a baby home, but believe me, change is still involved.

One of the first things to do before bringing me home is puppy proof our home and yard. The easiest way to do this is to walk from room to room, then from front yard to backyard with a critical eye. What you're looking for are trouble spots, dangerous things I can get into.

Put household cleaners *waaaaaay* out of my reach. The same goes for medication. Remember, I can chew right through childproof containers. Block electrical outlets and move your ash trays. *Better yet, stop smoking; it'll be better for both of us.*

Remember to put your sewing supplies away. I may swallow a pin or needle. *That probably feels even worse than it sounds and it sounds pretty awful.*

Please make sure I can't get to your indoor or outdoor trash cans, even though it would be sheer heaven for me.

Don't forget to screen off the fireplace and watch out for that weed killer in the garage and that small puddle of sweet-smelling, but deadly antifreeze on the driveway. Also, try to remember to keep your toilet seat down, because I won't understand why the water in that big white bowl is off-limits. Some of your beautiful houseplants will make me sick and could even kill me. I remember when one of our neighbors brought her two dogs home for the first time. She did a wonderful job of puppy proofing, but overlooked two things that put them in danger. The first one was a small rip in the bottom lining of her box spring mattress. One of her little dogs crawled in and was missing for hours. The neighbor searched her house from top to bottom several times in a panic. Before long she was crying, but luckily she heard his weak cries for help and was able to rescue him.

Here's a sampling of the plants you need to be sure I avoid:

caladium (elephant's ears)
dieffenbachia (dumb cane)
English ivy
hydrangea
Japanese yew
lily of the valley
oleander
philodendron
poinsettia
rhododendron (azalea)

The other close call involved her other puppy. It loved waking up early and exploring its new surroundings while she and the other doggie slept. One of the puppy's favorite things to do was get into the shower and lick the water droplets off the shower floor. She soon discovered that bars of soap were fun to lick too. She did this for several days, then started feeling really sick. Before long, the poor puppy started throwing up and soon was so weak and dehydrated that the neighbor thought it was going to travel to that great boneyard in the sky.

The vet couldn't figure out what was wrong with the puppy

You know, I never did understand this business about baths. Why, for centuries we dogs got along fine without anyone obsessing over giving us a bath. Now I'll just have to spend a bunch of time looking for something to roll in so I can get this awful soap smell off me.

—Penelope

and the only advice he could give our neighbor was to keep a close eye on her little dog and try to encourage it to eat. She did that and also held it close and cried. It weighed next to nothing. Even I thought its time was up. The next day this lady's brother came over to visit. He brought a pizza with him and I guess it smelled so good that the weak little puppy perked up a bit. When the lady noticed this, she hand-fed some teeny, tiny pieces of Canadian bacon topping to the puppy; the puppy ate very slowly and soon afterward took a big drink of water. That was the beginning of the end of the close call. Our neighbor didn't figure out what had made her puppy sick until several days later when she noticed small teeth marks on a bar of soap. After that, she always kept the shower door closed. I *know all this, because* I *heard the stories straight from the mouths of the dogs involved.*

So take my word for it, extensive puppy proofing of your home and yard will prevent headaches and heartaches later. It's simple, but vital.

In addition to puppy proofing, you'll want to have my bed ready before you bring me home. It's also a good idea to have my food and water dishes on hand. You can pick them up at just about any store. Homemade ones are fine too. As far as I'm concerned, a box with an old, warm blanket is just as cozy as a $45.00 dog bed, and old plastic bowls hold food and water just as well as store-bought, color-coordinated ones. But hey, it's your money, so the choice is yours.

After, or even before, you pick me up, pick out my name, and please don't keep changing it. You'll just confuse me, and believe me, I'm already confused and you can spell that with a capital "C." To make me feel more comfortable in my new home, have a little chew toy available. This will give me something to play with and will also increase the odds that you won't find my teeth marks on those shoes you forgot to put away while you were puppy proofing our home.

Please make sure the chew toy isn't one of your old tennis or racquet balls. If you let me play with these balls as a puppy, I'll think they're OK to play with as I grow older. You see, tennis and racquetballs are extremely dangerous. I can tear them apart and swallow the pieces, or worse, choke on the whole ball. *Picture that scene.* It's *ugly.*

You have to play detective next. Your assignment, if you choose to accept it, is to check out vets—you know, dog docs. As soon as you have selected a good, kind one, make an appointment for an initial checkup and vaccinations. For me, not you.

OK, OK, OK, I *was trying to be funny, but you're right, this is a* serious *subject*. Prepare yourself, when you first bring me home, I'll probably be homesick for awhile. This will be noticeable, especially at night. Get ready to put your pillow over your ears as you try to block out my whimpering and crying. But before you lose patience with me, please remember I've just been taken away from my family. The world as I know it has suddenly changed. I need a little time to get used to change.

There are ways to comfort me. One way would be to let me sleep with you. While I vote for this idea, I have to admit I'm a little biased, and it's probably not the best choice. Here's an old tried-and-true trick that works, but it hinges on finding an object that is fast becoming a thing of the past. I'm talking about a ticking clock. Nowadays, most clocks are digital, but in case you're lucky enough to find a ticking clock, wrap it in a warm blanket and let me sleep with it. I'll join the ranks of thousands of puppies throughout the years who have been fooled into believing the ticking is their mother's heartbeat.

Just to let you know, puppies, like human babies, sleep a lot, even 80 percent of the day, so don't worry when I spend most of my time napping. I'm not trying to mentally escape from my new environment. I'm just doing what comes naturally. Think of these as catnaps. *Get it? Catnaps. Come on; wag your tail*, OOPS, I mean smile, pleeeeeeease. See, that wasn't so bad.

Dog Talk

Did you know there's such a thing as a "dog language?" When I'm barking fast and furiously, that means there's something going on that I'm alerting you to. You're probably saying, "I knew that," but did you know that if you scratch my chest and baby talk to me, I'll lower my voice and make cooing sounds. Actually, it sounds like I'm yawning or humming, but I'm not; I'm chatting with you.

I can understand human speech too. English, Spanish, Japanese, it doesn't matter what language you use to speak to me. As

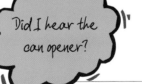
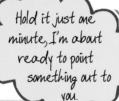

My human mom says I'm a little person with fur. But I know I'm a dog. And, although I speak fluent dog, I can also communicate with just a tilt of my head, a movement of my ears, a wag of my tail, or just that certain "look."

—Lizzie

a matter of fact, most dogs can understand several languages after a good deal of training. As for me, I'd love to bone up on Italian. The next time you leave me home alone, I plan to look through your books to see if there are any that can help me. *Don't worry, I won't make a mess. But if all goes well, you may find an Italian restaurant delivery truck in our driveway!*

While researchers all agree that I understand human words, they just can't agree on how many. As I mentioned earlier, some say my vocabulary averages 40 to 60 words; some say it can reach 300. I say it all depends on how much time you spend communicating with me.

I hate to brag, but I'm a quick learner. Just say the word, and then show me what you want me to do. I'll remember. Consistency is the key. As I mentioned earlier, I'm no dumb dog. I just memorize key sounds and gestures, then associate them with certain situations. It's called conditioning. *Don't be so amazed, you're conditioned too. Don't believe me? Try this. What do you picture when I say hot fudge sundae? I bet my life you're picturing a nice yummy treat, not a pickup truck or a palm tree.*

My brain works the same way. When you say "walk," I know what's coming. When you say "sit," I sit because you've taught me to. When you say "stay," I stay because I know that's what you want of me.

There is something I have to confess. I never, ever listen to your whole sentences. It's not that I don't care what you're saying, it's just that I'm smart enough to know the difference between key words and fluff. My mind quickly filters out the extra words and I connect the key words with subtle nonverbal cues. I *hope* I *haven't hurt your feelings*.

To make our lives easier, there are five words you should definitely teach me. Can you guess what they are? Here's a hint, they begin with the letters "h," "s," "d," "s," and "c." They're "heel," "sit," "down," "stay," and "come." It may take a little time to teach me what these words mean, but, hey, you didn't learn how to ride a bike the first time out either, did you?

I do have one small favor to ask of you to help from confusing me: please don't say the command twice within seconds. For example, please don't say "sit," then two seconds later yell "sit" again just because I'm not responding as fast as you'd like.

I can become confused when you "double talk" to me. It sounds like a totally different command, like "sit-sit."

For instance, wouldn't you become a little confused if someone someone started started talking talking to to you you like like this this. I *think you get the message*.

Before I wrap up this chapter, I want to share something with you that brings a smile to my face each time I think of it. On many occasions I have overheard you laughingly tell others that I have trained you, instead of you training me. If that were true, I'd be relaxing on a Lazy Boy with the TV on and a meat loaf sandwich within reach. I *love picturing that!*

• Is The Doctor In? •

Helpful Health Information

I s your HMO A-OK? I'm the first to agree that health care has really changed. For you, as well as for me. Nowadays, surgery is common for pets. A dog down the street had a kidney transplant that cost seven thousand dollars. *Don't worry, he's* OK. Other new treatments aimed at keeping me healthy include braces for my teeth as well as for broken bones, chiropractic therapy, swim therapy, aromatherapy, and acupuncture. I can even be given a prescription for my own version of Prozac to keep me calm when you leave me alone.

I'm grateful for these medical advancements. After all, my health is important to me, and I'm truly grateful that it's important to you too. In appreciation for your concern, I've put together the following "handy" health information.

What's Bugging You?—I Know What's Bugging Me

Fleas are those teeny, tiny creatures that give us both big headaches and, boy, do they reproduce. Listen to this, in one month ten adult fleas can produce 250,000 babies. I don't need a calculator to figure out that's big trouble.

Fleas love to see the sights. These wingless insects use me to get around; I guess you could say they think of me as a big plane, a 747. They love to rack up frequent flier miles. Their destinations: my bedding, your clean carpets, chairs, everywhere and anywhere. When they're done visiting, they hop back on me, and boy can they hop. The last time I went in for a vet visit, the dog doc was running a little late and I had some time to paw through a pamphlet put out by a flea-killing company called Defend. The pamphlet said fleas can jump 150 times the length of their bodies in any direction. If people had that ability, they could jump nearly 1,000 feet.

Also, if someone ever bets you he or she can catch a flea, get ready to win some fast money. The pamphlet said a flea accelerates almost 50 times faster than a space shuttle does at lift-off.

> **"I have to admit fleas are amazing creatures, but I hate them anyway."**

I have to admit fleas are amazing creatures, but I hate them anyway. And I know they're not a favorite of yours either. These annoying pests love to feed on my blood. I consider a flea a pint-size Dracula. It uses part of its mouth to grasp my skin, then it feeds away. That Defend pamphlet said a female flea can suck up to 15 times its body weight in blood daily. If that's not gross enough, fleas keep me scratching 24 hours a day.

The best way to win the flea-fight is to use the "triple attack battle plan." Treat the house, yard and me—all on the same day. Sounds like a big job, but it can be done. Take me in for a flea dip while a pest control company treats the yard and the house. My bedding should go into the wash that same day. If you're a little short on money and you decide to handle the "triple attack plan" yourself, I promise to help as much as I can.

When you treat the yard, you may want to use a solution designed to kill fleas in the larva stage. These products are called "insect growth regulators," or IGRs, and are reported to be safe around people and pets, but hey, you might want to check this out further; after all, years ago the U.S. government said asbestos was OK and even allowed its use in baby powder.

A couple of things you may want to check out are once-a-month flea pills for me and flea control skin drops, such as Advantage or Frontline Top Spot. Our vet can probably supply the latest safety data, but even I can tell you it's best to avoid putting a flea collar on me or submerging me in flea dip until I'm at least 15 weeks old. Remember, these chemicals are strong, and I admit they sometimes frighten me.

If chemicals don't scare you, sprinkle a small amount of flea powder on your carpet. If you vacuum up those pesky pests, they'll hang out in the bag and wait patiently for their chance to escape, so don't forget to change the bag often.

If chemicals make you nervous, like they make me nervous, remember this: fleas hate healthy dogs, and the healthier I am, the more natural oils are in my skin and coat. Those oils are big trouble for fleas, because these little parasites breathe through their bodies and my body oils can suffocate and kill them. So remember, just like a stake through a vampire's heart, one of the best ways to fight fleas is to keep me healthy.

Here's something else that helps avoid the use of chemicals. That old wives' tale that eucalyptus leaves in my bedding will help kill fleas is true, so feel free to add some of Mother Nature's natural brand of flea killer to my bedding. *If you're worried that the leaves will create a mess, I'd be more than happy to wear one of those new dog collars stuffed with eucalyptus leaves or one that contains eucalyptus oil.*

Tick Time

If you think fleas are a bad dream, ticks are a nightmare. When you find a tick on me, I know it repulses you, because whenever I see one, I feel like throwing up. Oh, *sorry*, I *don't mean that literally*. But please, muster up the courage and using a pair of tweezers, grasp any nasty tick you find on me as near to its head as you possibly can, then slowly and gently, using steady pressure, pull it out. You've probably heard it's a good idea to burn out a tick, but please don't. In addition to a tick problem, I don't need first, second, or third degree burns.

I hate to tell you this, but you should know—ticks can also make you sick, because they can pass on Lyme disease and Rocky Mountain spotted fever. You've probably read about Lyme disease in the newspaper. A few years ago it received a lot of media attention. I *know that everywhere I looked I saw something about it. I was really getting paranoid.*

Lyme Disease in Dogs

- How To Prevent the Problem

  Treat me and my environment with tick repellent; if you find a tick on me, remove it immediately

- What Symptoms To Watch For

  Sudden onset of limping, caused by painful, swollen joints; fever

- What To Do

  Take me to the vet

- What Our Vet May Suggest

  Antibiotics

Lyme disease is caused by a bacteria called Borrelia burgdorferi. I guess Borrelia is its first name and burgdorferi is its last name. OK, OK, I *was just trying to be funny, but, you're right once again; this is not the time for humor. I apologize.* If an infected tick bites you, a rash will break out at the bite site and you'll feel as if you have the flu. If you don't receive treatment, big trouble may be in store for you. You may end up with an inflamed heart, chronic arthritis, or problems with your nervous system.

I'm not affected as severely. I may experience overall weakness, lose my appetite, have trouble getting around due to swollen joints, and even develop arthritis, but it would be very unlikely that I would die from Lyme disease.

Please remember I can't pass on Lyme disease to you. Only an infected tick can do that. However, not all ticks transmit Lyme disease. The so-called "deer tick" is the primary carrier. In the United States, this tick is most commonly found in the northeastern, north central, and Pacific coastal states. If we live in one of these high-risk areas, check with our vet. You may want to have me vaccinated.

The Mighty Ear Mites

Another problem I might have is ear mites. Infected cats often contaminate me.

If you see me scratching my ears or shaking my head a lot, I'm not dancing to Three Dog Night. I might well have ear mites. Please take a peek. Hopefully, you won't see the telltale signs: dark ear wax or a substance that looks like coffee grounds or dried blood. But if you do, please take me to the vet. I'd really appreciate it.

Creepy Crawlers

Fleas, ticks and mites live on my skin, which makes them external parasites. There are internal parasites too. Internal parasites include worms that live inside a dog's body. I *know this stuff is gross, but it's important to know.* To tell you the truth, ignorance is actually as dangerous for you as for me, because many internal parasites fall under the category of zoonoses. No, I'm not making up that word. "My" dictionary says zoonotic diseases are illness that can be spread from animal to man. Before you start thinking I'm a walking health threat you don't want to be around, please let me point out that you can make me sick too! I didn't want to tell you this, but you've given me strep throat several times. Despite this, the thought of leaving you has never crossed my mind, and I hope after you read the following information, you'll feel the same way about having me around.

Roundworm is one of the things you can contract from me. I can contract roundworm from my mom during birth or while nursing. I can also pick it up by playing in areas where a lot of pets eliminate waste, such as parks. That's because tiny roundworm eggs live in infected soil, as well as in contaminated feces.

Roundworm is a long, thin parasite. A quick look at a puppy's stool will show telltale signs, but roundworm is a little trickier to detect in older dogs because they usually don't show symptoms. But don't worry, a vet will be able to tell if the dog is infected by peeking through a microscope at its stool. Roundworms will rarely jeopardize my life, but they do disrupt my body's adsorption of food and may stunt my growth.

If you're infected, the parasite may end up in some of your organs and tissues. That could mean permanent damage if you're not treated. Because of the threat to you, it's a good idea to have me undergo deworming treatment as a puppy, just to be on the safe side.

Two of the best ways to combat roundworm are to dispose of my feces on a regular basis and *always* wash your hands afterward.

Roundworm In Dogs

- How To Prevent the Problem

  Deworm me as a puppy, and clean up feces on a timely schedule

- What Symptoms To Watch For

  In puppies—potbellied appearance, dull coat, diarrhea, worms in stool; most infected adult dogs don't show symptoms

- What To Do

  Take me to our vet; avoid direct contact with my feces

- What Our Vet May Suggest

  Deworming medicine

Another zoonotic disease is heartworm. It comes from the bite of an infected mosquito. These worms like to live near my heart or major blood vessels. It's disgusting, I know. Heartworm can easily be avoided, since daily or monthly medication is available. I vote for the monthly dosage. Twelve pills a year can make all the difference in the world. Excessive cough is a symptom of infection, so if I cough a lot, you may want the vet to run a blood test on me to see if I have a heartworm infestation. Another symptom is if I suddenly become lethargic. It has nothing to do with laziness, and everything to do with the condition that is taking a serious toll on my body, so serious that it could cost me my life.

The "ABC's" Of "DHLP"

I receive protective antibodies from my mom, just like you did when you were a baby. These antibodies are delivered by my mother's first milk, which is called colostrum, just like your mother's. This natural immunity doesn't stay with me long though. It vanishes in about two weeks. So please remember that I'm susceptible to a number of diseases during the early weeks of my life. That's why it's best not to take me to visit your friends, go to public parks, or allow me to play with other dogs until I'm a little older. I know you just want to show me off, but I'll be safer at home during my first sixteen weeks of life. But *don't forget I need interaction for successful socialization, so be sure to spend some time with me.*

Just like human babies, I need shots to help keep me healthy. Vaccinations pick up where my mother's milk leaves off. The vet will probably give me what is called a "DHLP-parvo" shot. It will combat distemper, hepatitis, leptospirosis, parainfluenza and parvovirus. "DHLP" stands for the first letters in the first four words, get it?

Heartworm in Dogs

- *How To Prevent the Problem*

  Give me routine heartworm-fighting treatments; have our vet conduct periodic blood tests

- *What Symptoms To Watch For*

  Excessive coughing, trouble breathing, lethargy, weight loss

- *What To Do*

  Take me to our vet

- *What Our Vet May Suggest*

  Heartworm medication

Distemper is an airborne, highly contagious, often deadly virus that attacks my respiratory, gastrointestinal and nervous systems.

If I'm infected and lucky enough to survive distemper, I'll probably be scarred by the virus. And I'm not talking about scars a plastic surgeon can get rid of; I'm talking about nervous disorders such as a head tilt or uncontrollable tremors.

Hepatitis, which is officially called infectious canine hepatitis, will affect my liver, just like it does in humans. If my eyes turn blue, watch out, because I haven't started wearing colored contacts. Swelling of the cornea caused by hepatitis may be to blame. And, I hate to tell you this, but my eyes are the least of my problems; within hours I may just drop dead. It may happen so quickly that you may think I was poisoned, but it's just this horrible disease doing its dirty work.

Distemper

- How To Prevent the Problem

  Timely vaccinations

- What Symptoms To Watch For

  Rapid weight loss, diarrhea, vomiting, heavy discharge from eyes and nose, seizures

- What To Do

  Take me to our vet *immediately*

- What Our Vet May Suggest

  Antibiotics, seizure medication, vomiting and diarrhea medicine

Leptospirosis is no fun either. It's an extremely contagious disease. It's spread through an infected dog's nasal secretion, saliva, and urine. Dogs may also become infected by drinking standing water that has been contaminated by infected livestock or rodents. Leptospirosis can attack all body tissue but can especially damage my kidneys and liver.

Here's something to really stress you out; leptospirosis is a zoonotic disease. As I explained earlier, that means you can con-

Hepatitis

- *How To Prevent the Problem*

  Timely vaccinations

- *What Symptoms To Watch For*

  High fever; excessive thirst; heavy eye discharge; severe abdominal pain; hemorrhage from mouth, nose, or rectum; development of "blue eye"

- *What To Do*

  Take me to our vet immediately

- *What Our Vet May Suggest*

  Blood transfusion, antibiotics

tract leptospirosis too. So if you observe the symptoms of leptospirosis in me, be sure to contact your own doctor.

Parainfluenza virus commonly causes "canine cough or kennel cough." Viruses and bacteria are to blame for this airborne disease. This condition isn't as threatening as some of the other diseases I've been describing, but it sure can irritate my respiratory tract.

Canine cough is highly contagious, so if you bore me a lot, *oops, I mean board me a lot,*

please make sure my shots are up-to-date. Better yet, have our vet give me a "booster" shot.

The parvo part of the shot is also key to keeping me healthy. It combats what many dogs consider the canine version of the black plague. But this illness didn't pop up in the Middle Ages; it first struck in 1978. Researchers did develop a vaccine within three months,

Leptospirosis

- *How To Prevent the Problem*

  Timely vaccinations; don't let me drink from standing water when outdoors

- *What Symptoms To Watch For*

  Fever, vomiting, frequent urination, diarrhea

- *What To Do*

  Take me to our vet

- *What Our Vet May Suggest*

  Antibiotics, hospitalization and quarantine

Parainfluenza Virus

- *How To Prevent the Problem*

  Timely vaccinations; additional vaccination prior to boarding

- *What Symptoms To Watch For*

  Chronic cough

- *What To Do*

  Take me to our vet

- *What Our Vet May Suggest*

  Antibiotics, cough suppressant

but a year later dogs were still dying around the world and even today parvo is still a major threat to dogs, especially to puppies younger than six months. That's because this disease is highly contagious. You see, the stools of sick dogs carry parvovirus, which in turn contaminates exposed soil. The virus can live in the soil for at least five months and sometimes longer. So, if I walk through an infected area, I can pick up parvo on my paws. The same goes for you, except you don't pick it up on your paws, you carry the virus home on the soles of your shoes. It can also be carried to our home on the soles of our mail carrier, visiting friends, the pizza delivery guy; you get the picture.

It's not uncommon for this intestinal virus to wipe out entire litters. One day the puppies look fine, hours later, they're dying. To make matters worst, there's no magic drug for this dreaded disease once it hits. All you can do is get me to the vet as soon as possible and pray. I hope you never have to witness this disease on its merciless rampage; it will break your heart. I really mean that.

Parvo

- *How To Prevent the Problem*

  Timely vaccinations

- *What Symptoms To Watch For*

  Rapid decline in health

- *What To Do*

  Take me to our vet immediately

- *What Our Vet May Suggest*

  Immediate hospitalization

Rabid Rabies

It's the law of the land: rabies shots on a regular basis are a must, no two ways about it. That's because you can't play around with this deadly disease. Rabies is a viral disease that affects the brain.

This disease is contracted through the bite of an infected mammal. Possible carriers include bats, raccoons, foxes, and skunks.

I should get my first rabies vaccination at 12 months to 16 months. The potency of the vaccine determines how long I'm protected. Then I will need another vaccination in one year and then another every one to three years, depending on state regulations. And remember, this is another disease humans can contract, so it's extremely important that I'm protected.

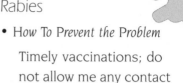

Rabies

- **How To Prevent the Problem**

  Timely vaccinations; do not allow me any contact with wild animals

- **What Symptoms To Watch For**

  Withdrawal, drooling, inability to swallow, violent behavior, sensitivity to noise, foaming at the mouth

- **What To Do**

  Do not approach me; contact animal control officer

- **What Animal Control Officer May Suggest**

  Euthanasia, brain tissue tested for rabies

Hachoo!

I notice some humans sneeze when they're around me. I feel badly about this. People may think they're allergic to my fur, but that's really not the case at all. Dog allergens are found in my dander. Dander is the dry scales released from my skin. But, I'm the first to admit this information doesn't change the bottom line, and that's the fact that someone is sneezing because of me. Before you send me packing, please do some research to see if my

After a long day of roping cattle, my human dad and I jumped into our pickup truck and, since he looked so tired, I volunteered to drive. He looked at me and shook his head. I guess he knew I didn't have my driver's license with me.
—Dallie

dander is really the cause of the problem. If it is, there are some things we can do. Number one is beefing up my grooming. I *love that word, beefing, don't you?*

Someone who isn't allergic to my dander should brush my fur each day outdoors. If that's too much of a time commitment, have that person reach for the vacuum cleaner and turn the attachment on me. The first time I'm vacuumed, I probably will try to run, but please don't get upset with me, because you probably wouldn't sit still the first time someone vacuumed you. But more likely, after a while I'll like being vacuumed. It may even become a favorite part of my day. Another thing you may want to try is adding a small amount of vegetable oil, such as olive or safflower oil, to my diet each day. Essential fatty acids in these oils help keep my coat healthy, which, in turn, cuts down on shedding. Placing an air filter in our house may also help, as well as regularly washing my bedding. If worse comes to worse, make me an "outside" dog. I know I'll miss being in the house, but, hey, as long as I know you're close, it's OK.

I sneeze too; I know you've heard me. Sorry, I keep forgetting to cover my mouth with my paws, but I'll try to remember my manners next time.

An occasional sneeze is normal, especially if, as I mentioned earlier during our walk, I get a big whiff of perfume or cologne, but if I start to sneeze uncontrollably and can't stop, a foxtail or some other type of burr may be lodged in my nose. Don't just hand me a box of tissues; please take me to the vet so it can be removed. By the way, foxtails and other burrs can also irritate my ears. However, when that happens I don't sneeze!

When To Reach For The Car Keys

Vet visits aren't cheap; I know that because the last time you took me to the vet, I peeked over your shoulder as you were writing the check to pay the bill. To save you some money, here are some rough guidelines to help determine when it's truly "trouble time."

Keep a close eye on me if I seem to lack energy, thumb my nose at a favorite treat, throw up occasionally or have loose stools. If I'm not back to normal in several hours, call the dog doc and describe my symptoms. The vet will tell you what to do.

Please call the vet immediately if I have bloody diarrhea, bloody urine or throw up continuously.

Please, please, please take me immediately to the vet if I'm bleeding seriously, pass out, suffer seizures, eat or drink something poisonous, or if I'm suffering from a superbad case of the runs. Also, if my lips, mouth or throat swell and I can't breathe easily, it's time to grab the car keys and head to the vet's office. I may have been stung by a bee or wasp and I might be experiencing an allergic reaction that could kill me.

I'm tiny, with only a nine-pound frame, but I just love to chase cats and anything else that moves. My human dad says I'm fearless. He says that's what attracted him to me when he was dog-shopping at the pound. And I love to eat. Especially steak and pasta. But I mainly get dog food. Grrrrrr.
—Falena

If I'm hit by a car and manage to walk away from the accident scene, don't consider it a miracle until a vet checks me out. I might have internal injuries that could prove deadly.

As I said, I know these visits can put a dent in your already dented pocketbook. Health insurance for dogs does exist. You may want to look into it. After all, just about any medical procedure that is available to humans can be performed on me.

Are you feeling a little overwhelmed, with too much information to remember? Don't worry, I'll sum it up for you. I should get my shots regularly and be checked periodically for worms and other parasites. This all can be done during a yearly vet visit. The best thing about this is that at least once a year I get to ride in the car. I *loooooooove riding in our car.*

• My Sex Life •

Don't Worry, I Won't Make You Blush

Do you remember back in grade school when girls and boys were divided into groups and given that awkward first sex education lesson? Well, here's a little lesson on my sex life. Don't worry, I'll try my best not to make you blush.

I'm going to start our lesson with a little background on wolves. In each pack usually only the alpha wolf mates, and his bride is the dominant female—no matter if he thinks she's cute or not. This instinctive restriction on mating leads to fewer mouths to feed. This increases the odds that each litter of pups will survive, but it also leads to a lot of sexually frustrated male wolves who spend a lot of time trying to become the leader of the pack.

I hate to admit it, but a lot of male dogs also have lousy sex lives. You see, most male dogs reach sexual maturity at six months of age, and then they're always ready for a romp. Six-months and older female dogs, on the other hand, go into heat about twice a year. These heat periods are usually equally spaced throughout the year and last approximately 21 days. These periods consist of three states: proestrus, estrus, and diestrus. Estrus is considered "true heat" and lasts for about five days. It's the only time a female will willingly accept a male. Now, wasn't that a nice way of phrasing things? I've decided the timing of the male and female sex drives is Mother Nature's way of promoting birth control. Just think what would happen if male and female dogs spent all their time having sex. There would be way too many puppies.

Back to our lesson. Just before estrus, the female dog will pee more frequently. She's leaving sexy scented messages that will lead male dogs to her.

You would think that during estrus, when the female is ready and willing, male dogs nearby would be in sheer heaven. Wrong! Usually more frustration awaits, because, admit it, the last thing you want me to do is have sex with the dog down the street.

If I am lucky enough to escape from the yard and make a date, you may see me and my partner locked together. Don't reach for a stick and try to separate us. Nothing unnatural is happening; the mating process just hasn't reached completion. You see, after ejaculation, the base of the penis swells inside the female. It may stay that way for more than 30 minutes. I have shuddered at the sight of people turning the hose on mating dogs, but this is unnecessary; the lovers will disengage themselves naturally in their own good time.

By the way, I can mate with any breed of dog. Size might make it almost physically impossible, but biologically it can happen. And yes, those jokes are true; I can mate with such animals as wolves and coyotes. And since I'm coming clean on this sensitive subject matter, yes, male dogs are trying to get some sexual satisfaction when they hump your leg. And, some researchers think male dogs especially love it when you scratch their chests, because the scratching resembles the sensation they feel during doggy romance.

Male dogs aren't the only ones who are frustrated. Female dogs are also facing severe sexual problems in our modern world. As I mentioned just a bit ago, in the world of wolves, usually only

I can't remember when this was taken. It was either on a day when I was dog-tired or it was during the dog days of summer.

—Katie

the alpha female gets to mate and have pups. Other females in the pack help raise the pups, but they usually don't get to experience motherhood firsthand. Nowadays, many female dogs are also prevented from becoming pregnant. This can be rough. It sometimes triggers something called pseudopregnancy, which is a fancy word for false pregnancy. The female thinks she's pregnant, and she becomes physically and mentally ready to give birth. But instead of puppies, all she gets is disappointment. This can happen over and over and over again with each heat cycle, leading to confusion and stress.

When a female does become pregnant, her pregnancy is called gestation. It averages nine weeks, *which sure beats the nine-month hu-*

man gestation period, don't you think? Any mom-to-be should be checked out by a vet. As time for delivery nears, make available a couple of empty boxes with clean blankets in them so that she can choose her own birthing place.

When born, after emerging from my mother, my body is encased in a transparent sac. My mom sets me free by using her teeth to tear this sac open, and then she quickly begins to lick my body to jump-start my lungs. Mom's salvia is a little sticky, but I'm so busy trying to breathe, I don't mind. As soon as my breathing stabilizes, she bites off and swallows my umbilical cord. All I can say is I'm glad she knows what she's doing, because I have no idea what's going on. Mother Nature allows her to spend about half an hour soothing my fears before another puppy begins to emerge, and she begins the birthing process again, and again, and again,

> **❝ A favorite spot for puppies to catch some zzzz's is in their pile of littermates. They provide warmth and security to each other like no security blanket ever could.❞**

and again. Five puppies is the average number in a litter. *Just imagine quintuplets as an average delivery.*

Remember, that although newborn puppies are cute, they are tiny and fragile, and they need their mom's attention, rather than human attention and grabbing hands.

As I mentioned, as puppies we really aren't aware of our surroundings during this early part of our lives. In fact, we usually don't even open our eyes during the first two weeks of life. Instead of exploring, we spend most of our time sleeping, because the part of our brain that controls wakefulness is still developing. A favorite spot for puppies to

I have this one particular doggy toy that I am just crazy about. It's a hard rubber ball. Everyday I play a rousing game of room rugby with it, but unfortunately it always ends up rolling under the couch. So the pose in this picture—taken by my human mom who thought I was asleep—is pretty typical of part of my daily routine.
—Soda Pop

catch some zzzz's is in their pile of littermates. They provide warmth and security to each other like no security blanket ever could. If a puppy isn't sleeping, it's eating. You may have noticed that new-born kitties will search out a certain teat to feed from, but puppies aren't that picky; they'll just reach for the closest.

Here's something I find really interesting: one aspect of my nursing stage stays with me for life. As a puppy I learned to knead the teat with my tiny paws when I wanted milk, and now later in life I extend my paws forward when I want something. That's why it's so easy for you to teach me to shake hands. *And you thought you were just a great trainer!*

About 15 days into my life, my hearing kicks in. *Let me tell you the first time I heard a sound, it wasn't music to my ears. I really freaked out, having no idea what was going on.* I quickly calmed down though, because a puppy's innate curiosity soon has it exploring and enjoying its new life. When puppies reach two to three weeks of age, they begin to generate body heat more efficiently, so much, in fact, that they usually prefer to sleep in rows rather than in piles. *But don't worry, my affection for cuddling stays with me for life!*

Puppies will continue to develop rapidly during the first six months, when male and female puppies reach sexual maturity. Since we can't use condoms or take birth control pills, humans have come up with other means of controlling our reproduction.

Birth Control

Spaying is a procedure performed on a female dog. It's officially called ovariohysterectomy. In a nutshell, it means the female's reproductive organs are removed. Anesthetic is used to put her under, then abdominal surgery takes place. After spaying, a female dog will no longer experience heat cycles, *but she will have a scar on her tummy.*

Neutering usually refers to the castration of a male dog. To put it plainly, his testicles are cut off. Neutering is also performed under general anesthesia. *Thank goodness, because I can't even envision the possibility of being conscious.* Now, what I'm going to tell you next may be hard to believe, but it's true. Canine testicular cosmetic implants are available. *Humans think of everything!*

When spaying and neutering take place, they are done deals—irreversible surgical procedures. The procedures may sound harsh, but here's the shocking and sad factual alternative: each and every year, millions and millions and millions of dogs and puppies are left at animal shelters. Many of the people dropping them off fool themselves by thinking their unwanted pets are going to find new homes, but that's often not the case, since more than half never find new homes and have to be destroyed. That's a nice way of saying *killed. Think about that, and whatever you do, don't ignore Mother Nature and allow doggy overpopulation to occur in your household and neighborhood. Please.*

• First Class, Please •

Traveling With Me

Did you know I could fly? I prefer first class, but I always seem to end up in the cargo bay. Most airlines do allow pets to travel. Some consider us "excess baggage"; others will allow you to put me in a carrier under your seat, that is, of course, if I'm small enough. Each airline is different, so you need to make several calls before you buy your ticket. There are federal rules all airlines must meet, and one is that pets can't be kept where temperatures are above 85 or below 45 degrees Fahrenheit. That's because temperatures will fluctuate greatly during flight. I could freeze, or I could bake. *Neither sounds appealing.*

Just to prepare you, you'll also have to deal with crate specifications and health and immunization certificate requirements.

Keep in mind, direct flights are better; after all, dogs can get lost just like luggage. But *I'm easier to find because I can bark and your clothes can't.*

If you decide you don't want to take me along, I'll understand. You can just leave me home alone with a big bag of dog food. *Forty pounds should do the trick.* Or, you can try conning our neighbors into coming over to feed me. *I'm positive they've forgotten*

my little poop in their pansies by now. You may also want to consider a professional pet sitter, or you can bore me, I mean board me. *Oh, I guess I already used that joke!*

Guess what I vote for. Give me a "k" ... give me an "e"... give me an "n." Have you guessed where I want to go? If you guessed, "Kentucky," you're wrong, guess again...you're right, a kennel. *Oops, I forgot it's passé to call them kennels. Today, kennels are called pet resorts, pet camps, or canine country clubs.* These places are big business, and that's with a capital "B." Get ready to shell out anywhere from $7.50 per day to $1,500 per week. But, hey, when you're lying on the beach in Hawaii, you won't feel so guilty when you think of me. I'll be relaxing with my own canine companions.

> **"** I know I love to ride in the back of pickup trucks. It's fun, but dangerous, so don't let me, no matter how much I beg. **"**

Too Hot To Handle

My normal body temperature ranges from 100.5 to 102.5 degrees Fahrenheit and I'd like to keep it that way, *so please, please, please, don't leave me in the car during warm weather while you run an errand, even a quick one.* It's like leaving your child in the oven. I'm not kidding! On a hot day the temperature inside a parked car can soar to over 155 degrees in minutes, and I do mean minutes. The heat can cause brain damage, even kill me. Being trapped in a hot car is a danger for anybody, but I'm in real trouble because the only way I can fight the heat is by panting, which allows me to breathe in air that has been slightly cooled by my wet tongue. You sweat, but I don't. My only efficient sweat glands are on the bottom of my paws, and let me tell you, they don't do the trick.

So panting is the only game in town for me, and the faster I

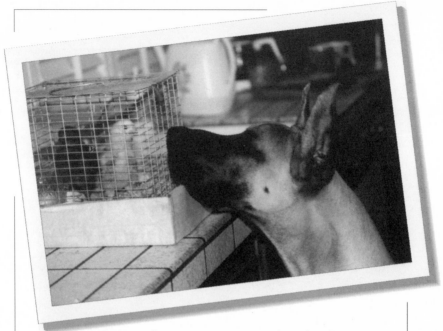

Everybody really seems to get antsy when they first meet me, and I'm really not sure why, because I am as friendly as they come. These chicks don't seem too concerned, though, but I guess they've getting sort of a limited perspective of me.
—Duke

pant in hopes of cooling off while in a car, the more danger my life is in.

Since we're on the subject of heat and cars, I know I love to ride in the back of pickup trucks. It's fun, but dangerous, so don't let me, no matter how much I beg. In the summer, the floor of a flatbed becomes scorching hot. Picture walking barefoot on hot asphalt. My foot pad leather offers some protection, but my constant pacing is proof that the situation can easily become too hot to handle.

Pacing also increases the odds that I'll take the big tumble and fall out of the pickup bed. Last I heard, the Humane Society

I'm Jo Jo, and I'm pictured here with my daughter, Tasha, and son, Sidney. This is one of my favorite pictures of my family. My kids are a lot like me, except for one thing, I love riding in cars, the longer the trip, the better. The two of them hate traveling. They always get carsick. They must have gotten that from their dad's side of the family.

—Jo Jo

of the United States said about 100,000 dogs are killed this way each year. *That's one list I don't want to be on.*

Riding in the back of a pickup also increases the danger that I'll get dirt and bugs in my eyes. These small particles can cause big problems. So please, just tell me "no" when I ask to tag along. Better yet, get one of those new seat belt attachments designed for dogs and let me ride up front with you. Or just leave me at home.

That Box Goes Over There

When you decide to stick a "For Sale" sign in front of our home, don't worry, I won't give you as much trouble as a cat will when it comes to leaving our old house behind. You see, one of the big differences between cats and dogs is that finicky felines have a tendency to prefer places over people.

> **❝** You see, one of the big differences between cats and dogs is that finicky felines have a tendency to prefer places over people. **❞**

That's not the case when it comes to dogs. I'll go anywhere with you. If you don't believe me and you feel like pretending to be Ben Franklin, here's a little test you can conduct. The next time it's raining and I'm inside, stand outside and call me to you. I may hesitate just a bit because of the wet weather. But, hey, if you want to stand in the rain, *what the heck!* I'll stand out there right along with you. We'll be wet, but we'll be together.

Here's a little reminder: when we move, please don't forget to obtain new dog tags for me as soon as possible. I'd appreciate it. My name and your phone number is sufficient, no need to put our address on the tags; what with the threat of crime and everything, it's best to be extra careful these days.

Since we're on the subject of dog tags, you may want to

check my collar. If you can't slip the width of two fingers under my collar, it's too tight and it's time to get me a new one—a buckled or snap-on one, please. Those new collars on the market that flash in the dark are cool too. Another caution: don't ever put a choke collar on me when I'm unsupervised. That's like letting your child play with a loaded gun. I can easily get it caught on something and choke myself to death.

If dog collars are too old-fashioned for you, you can try registration implants or tattoos to keep track of me. A little kitty tattoo on my ankle would be nice. *Just kidding*!

• Kibbles & Tidbits •

Interesting Dog Facts

And In This Corner Is...

We all know there are "dog people" and there are "cat people." The difference between the two groups is huge, and that's because dogs and cats are very different. Dogs are loyal, lovable, lively, and loads of fun. On top of that, we're cuter than cats.

Cats are selfish, stuck-up, standoffish. OK, OK, OK, I *guess I'm a little biased*. This dog versus cat battle has been going on for a long time and you can see which side I'm rooting for. In my opinion and for what it's worth, cats are just too darn independent. But, hey, I guess some people like that quality when it comes to choosing their pets. I've heard cat lovers say dogs need so much human attention. I guess that's true. My favorite part of the day is when I'm with you.

I hate to admit it, but cats outnumber dogs as pets. However, the last time I counted, I came up with about 150 million dogs worldwide that share their lives with people. Cats don't actually share their lives with people; they own them. *No, you don't have to reread the sentence, I said people are owned by cats.*

Don't worry, I'm not planning on chewing the shoes, I'm just hiding from Bo, my bulldog big brother. My human mom says I'm quite the character; she says I'm very dramatic and if I were a person, I'd probably be an actress. I think I'd be a school teacher. I already happen to know how the word "treat" is spelled. You see, my human parents thought if they spelled the word, I wouldn't know what they were talking about, but I caught on a long time ago!
—Bridgette

Some people say cats are cool, but try jogging with one. It's a little tough. As for me, I make a great jogging partner; in fact, I'm always ready and willing to take a jog, even on the days when you aren't up to it.

Cats also aren't very affectionate. How many cats greet their owners with big kisses when they return home? Most cats I know, and I know a lot, will wait until they're good and ready for some human contact before they even say hello.

While dog and cat people have their differences, the gap is like night and day when it comes to pet people and nonpet people.

Try telling a nonpet person that you kiss me when you come home, and I'll bet you a nice beefy bone it will gross them out. They'll also think you're a little strange when they find out you carry a picture of me in your wallet. And, they'll really think you're weird when they discover you sign greeting cards from me, talk to me on the phone, buy me birthday and holiday gifts, hang a Christmas stocking for me, and even rearrange furniture so I can look out of our windows. But hey, don't stop doing these things—I love

> **"Some people say cats are cool, but try jogging with one."**

them—don't worry that nonpet people don't understand. They're the ones missing out on a unique relationship.

I will tell you that some nonpet people do have a change of heart once they get to know us dogs better. When one of our neighbors first brought her new puppies home, that neighbor's mother didn't like them at all. When she visited our neighbor, she told her things like: "Dogs belong outside"; "Dogs don't need treats"; "Dogs are dirty." She hurt the puppies' feelings and they tried to keep their distance from her, but they still wagged their tails and hoped for acceptance each time she came over. Now, nine years later, the lady loves those dogs. Each week she cleans out her refrigerator and brings them the leftovers. The last time their human mom was out of town and "grandma" was dog-sitting, she actually made pasta soup especially for them. They told me it was warm and wonderful and they also said "So is she."

9 To 5

As you know, most dogs don't have outside careers. But that wasn't always the case. Years ago just about all of us were "working" dogs. Even today some lucky canines do have outside careers. A few are actors, some search for lost people, still others track illegal drugs.

Police work is a big draw for dogs. Just about every police department has a canine unit. It's challenging and exciting work, and the only negative thing about a career in law enforcement is we dogs don't get to wear badges. But *maybe that's a good thing because pinning them on would probably hurt.*

Some of us serve in the military and believe me, we're not playing ball with the troops; we're out on the front lines, searching for explosives and guarding base perimeters. Sometimes, in order to get to those front lines we even have to parachute out of planes. Our involvement with the military goes back thousands of years. The Romans used mastiff dogs as warriors and gladiators. These fighting dogs wore suits of armor and collars trimmed with razor-sharp daggers. Alexander the Great counted dogs among his troops. During World War II, the British used dogs to help find wounded soldiers, and the U.S. Army formed its famous K-9 unit. We were also drafted for the Vietnam War and did our duty in the Gulf War.

I personally was hoping to become an astronaut, but jobs in the space exploration field are harder to find than the Big Dipper on a cloudy night. But back in 1957, the Russians put a stray dog by the name of Laika on board Muttnik II, *oops*, I mean Sputnik II. Laika was the first living creature to orbit earth. A*nd, in case you're wondering, in English Laika means barker, and there was probably plenty of barking going on in that spacecraft, but luckily no neighbors were around to complain!*

Dogs are also important players in the health field. As I mentioned earlier, some of us aid the blind by becoming guide dogs, others assist the hearing-impaired, and some dogs are even trained to warn epileptics of upcoming seizures.

Animal testing is something else we're used for, and although I hate to talk about the subject, I do want to tell you about a history-making event that involved medicine and dogs. Back in 1925, an Alaskan malamute named Balto helped save many lives. Balto led a dogsled team into Nome, Alaska, after his master became snow-blind. The team carried a precious cargo, diphtheria antiserum, across about 1,150 miles of nature's coldest, harshest terrain. The serum saved people in that area from a medical epidemic. The annual Iditarod trail sled dog race commemorates the event. If you don't believe me, the next time you're in New York City, stop by Central Park, where you'll find a statue dedicated to good old Balto.

As I mentioned a bit ago, dogs serve in the military, but it seems we don't handle guns very well. There's a dog in Manitoba, Canada, who accidentally shot his owner with a .22 caliber rifle. I'm not kidding; I read about it in a newspaper. The article reported the owner was setting the sight and scope on his loaded gun with the safety off. When he walked over to adjust his target, his dog, named Vegas, bumped against the gun and it went off. The bullet hit the owner right in his back. The dog didn't run away and hide. It ran to its unconscious owner, licked and pawed at him until he came to, then dragged him from the backyard to a deck where the wounded owner was able to call 911. There is a happy ending to this story; the owner recovered and he didn't get rid of Vegas. He says he was stupid for handling the gun like that and considers his dog a hero for rescuing him. *Now, that's my kind of story—and owner.*

Believe It Or Not

One day when you weren't home, I found an old Trivial Pursuit game way back in the closet. I tried playing, but I didn't do so well. *Hey, I have to do something to keep busy all those hours when you're not home!* I put it neatly away, and I'm now hoping the manufacturers will come out with a dog version of the game. I know I'd do well because my mind is filled with dog trivia. For instance, did you know there's a museum dedicated to dogs? It's located in St. Louis and is called the American Kennel Club Museum of the Dog. It's nestled on 300 acres and is filled with 2,000 pieces of art inspired by dogs. If you're ever in the area, stop by and check out the collection of silver and brass dog collars. I've heard it's pretty nice. And please, don't forget to send me a postcard. *I'm trying to develop a better relationship with our mail carrier.*

Did you know we have a star named after us? No, *it's not on the Hollywood Walk of Fame.* It's Sirius, the dog star. When the Romans ruled, they called the hottest weeks in summer "the dog days." They thought the placement of the star had something to do with the heat. It doesn't, but, hey, it goes to prove humans aren't always right.

Since we're on the subject of stars, the dog plays a big part in the Chinese zodiac. Every 12 years comes the Year of the Dog. That means if you're born in 1922, 1934, 1946, 1958, 1970, 1982, 1994, 2006, or 2018, you're my celestial soul mate. Ancient Chinese astrologers determined the people born during the Year of the Dog are honest and loyal, which doesn't surprise me at all.

In modern-day China dogs are rare. Overcrowding has led to restrictions on pet ownership and many pet lovers are forced to visit zoos just to see dogs, or they can even rent dogs by the hour.

The picture isn't much brighter in Japan. Many Japanese dog lovers actually resort to buying robotic dogs. And, let me tell you, robotic dogs are not cheap. Each costs about $2,000. But at least the owners save money on dog food, which, by the way, in Japan is mostly made of fish.

Spending time with us dogs is something humans all over the world like to do. But I must admit I was pleasantly surprised when the dog across the street told me that a poll by the American Animal Hospital Association found that 57 percent of pet owners surveyed would choose to be shipwrecked on a desert island with their pet rather than with another person.

The dog across the street also told me about a dog by the name of Randy who didn't have to be shipwrecked to face a watery ordeal. He fell into a neighbor's Doughboy pool and had to tread water for at least 18 hours before being found. *Talk about dog paddling!*

Since we're on the subject of pools, did you know that a lot of dogs own their own wading pools; you may know the ones I'm talking about—those blue, hard-plastic ones sold for kids. Nothing beats lying in one filled with a little water on a hot summer day. *But don't forget to empty it when I'm done playing. The water can pose a drowning danger to the neighborhood kids.*

Here's another item from the "hard to believe" file: For $10,000 dollars you can have my DNA frozen and stored so that I can be cloned in the future. *All I ask is that you don't forget to pay the $100 annual storage fee!*

And here's another chilly fact: Anchorage, Alaska, has the most dogs per capita of any U.S. city. In all honesty, I have no idea why. But I am aware of a new breed of dog that doesn't mind cold temperatures. They're computer creatures. These man-made virtual reality puppies don't mind being confined to computers. As for me, I love running free outdoors and don't ever plan to do anything that would land me in dog court. *There really is one. It's in San Francisco.*

Here's a final piece of dog trivia. There is a growing market for dog perfume. Yes, if you search, you will find canine cologne. Feel free to pick up a bottle for me.

See, I told you I was an expert on dog trivia. *If the dog version of Trivial Pursuit doesn't come through, maybe I can get on Jeopardy. I can't wait to say "Dogs for $300."*

Unsolved Mysteries

I know you've heard the story, or one similar to it: "Dog Travels More Than 1,000 Miles To Find Owner Who Moved." While you may find these stories hard to believe, I don't. I think I have a natural homing ability, an internal compass, that leads me where I need to be.

I also have other unexplained talents. Scientists with video cameras have proven time and time again that I begin to anticipate your arrival, even when you're working irregular hours. It's strange, but true. You need to accept the fact that I can sense when you're coming home.

Scientists have also documented that I get a little shaky just before earthquakes. They wonder if it's because I sense changes in magnetic fields or hear the earth move.

Before you become frightened about these unexplained talents, think about it for a second; humans have five wonderful senses, but maybe we dogs have extra senses or the senses we do have are just so much sharper than those of humans that they seem inexplicable, *good word, huh; it's that missing dictionary once again*. Picture it this way: assume that no one else on earth but you can see. Try explaining your sense of sight to people who have never experienced such a wonder. It would be incredibly difficult for them to understand your ability. Many would be afraid of you and consider you strange.

Please remember, the human body enables you to do amazing things, so why shouldn't my body enable me to do amazing stuff too. When it comes to spreading out talent, I've noticed Mother Nature is pretty fair.

• *Happy Birthday To Me!* •

Yes, Those Are Wrinkles Under My Fur

Just like humans and everything else on this earth, I age. *You just can't see my wrinkles because of all my fur. Just kidding.* Since my life span is shorter than yours is, I age more rapidly. People used to think one year of my life equals seven human years. Well, people who study this kind of thing say there's more to it than that.

I grow most rapidly in the first two years of my life. During those 24 months, I will grow from a puppy to the equal of about 24 human years. For each year after the first two, add four years to approximate my age in human years. Take a look at the chart on the next page; it will help you understand my aging process.

Unfortunately, the bigger I am physically, the shorter my life span. You can expect small breeds (20 pounds and under) to live up to 13 years, medium-sized dogs (21 to 50 pounds) to live up to eleven and a half years, large breeds (51 to 90 pounds) to live up to ten and a half years, and dogs that weigh over 100 pounds will usually live up to seven and a half years. I do want to let you know that advances in veterinarian medicine, as well as canine nutrition, are paying off. The length of my life span is slowly but steadily

Dog — Human Age Comparison Chart

Dog	Human
6 months	10 years
8 months	13 years
10 months	14 years
12 months	15 years
18 months	20 years
2 years	24 years
4 years	32 years
6 years	40 years
8 years	48 years
10 years	56 years
12 years	64 years
14 years	72 years
16 years	80 years
18 years	88 years
20 years	96 years
21 years	100 years

increasing. All I have to say about that is WOW, *oops*, I *mean* BOW-WOW! By the way, cats are luckier; they live on the average of 16 to 20 years. Birds may live 30 years or more.

But for many of us, the passage of time still brings the same type of ailments that many older humans experience, such as arthritis. I hate to admit it, but the years do slow me down.

Maybe my short life span is the reason I choose to fill my life with love...no time for hate, no time for grudges, no time for prejudices.

I sure wish I could read. Because if I could I'd look up "lemur" in a book about animals and maybe I could figure out why the ninth-grade science teacher who lives next door always says to me, "Come 'mer, you little lemur, you!"

—Littledog

More Reasons To Have Me Around

I know having me around can sometimes be a pain, because I've seen you lug 40-pound bags of dog food out of our car often enough. And I know picking up dog doo-doo is no fun. But my presence is good for you, really it is.

Did you know your blood pressure drops when you pet me. So after a stressful day at work, consider reaching for me, rather than a drink.

Also, heart attack patients live longer if they have pets. We all know seniors who have pets are happier, but did you know kids who grow up with pets get a head start on learning responsibility and how to love.

Saying Goodbye

I don't know if there's a "dog heaven," just as you may wonder if there's a "human heaven."

But I do hope heaven exists, and I hope it's the same heaven for both of us, because I do want to see you again.

When I die, don't be afraid or embarrassed to mourn for me just because I'm only a dog. Our love is real.

When I die, you may experience several emotions: shock, denial, depression, anger, hopelessness, and finally acceptance. These feelings may last for a short time or for a long time. Don't be afraid to talk with someone about them.

Just remember I love you, and I want what's best for you. Tuck my memory into your heart and treasure our time together, but please live each day to its fullest. Remember I want you to be happy. Nothing brings me more pleasure than your smile. You know that.

When you're ready to get another dog, don't feel guilty. Just don't expect that dog to be me. Love it for itself. Each dog has its own personality and spirit. Each is unique. There is no other like it on earth. Just as there is no other person like you.

What I Really Want to Say to You

I'm Your Best Friend

I'll never know how the stock market works or why DVDs supply a clearer picture. But I do know I love you. I love you no matter how rich you are, no matter how poor. I love you when you're healthy and when you're sick. I love you when friends abound and when everybody deserts you. If you have a bad day at work, I'm there to listen. If tragedy strikes, I do my best to lick away the tears. I also do by best to protect you from danger. You know I'd lay down my life for you without a moment's hesitation. I try to make you smile and I turn your house into a home. When it comes to loyalty and love, few humans can measure up to me.

One Last Thing

It was nice talking with you, but now it seems that I'm losing my voice, so please come closer so that I can whisper something in your ear. I just want to tell you one last thing before I lose my ability to speak, and it's the most important, it's the first thing I shared with you: I *love you unconditionally.*

I'll always be on your side and by your side. No matter what life holds for you; if you allow me to, I'll happily walk the path of life with you.

Please take a moment to think about that.

Take care. I *love you.*

—Your Dog

Resources

Organizations

American Humane Association
63 Inverness Drive East
Englewood, CO 80112
303-792-9900
http//www.americanhumane.org

American Kennel Club
5580 Centerview Drive, Suite 200
Raleigh, NC 27606-3390
919-233-9767
http://www.aka.com

American Society for the Prevention of
Cruelty to Animals
424 E. 92nd Street
New York, NY 10128
212-876-7700
www.aspca.org
Check the Yellow Pages under "Animal
Shelters" or "Humane Society" for a
shelter near you

American Veterinary Medical Association
www.avma.org

Doris Day Animal League
227 Massachusetts Avenue NE, Suite 100
Washington, DC 20002
202-546-1761
ddal@aol.com

Greyhound Pets of America
800-366-1472

Humane Society of the United States
2100 L Street NW
Washington, DC 20037
202-452-1100
http://www.hsus.org

National Association of Professional Pet
Sitters
800-296-PETS
http://www.petsitters.org

National Dog Registry
800-NDR-DOGS

NetVet Veterinary Resources
http://www.avma.org/netvet

North American Flyball Association
1400 W. Devon Avenue #512
Chicago, IL 60660
http://www.flyball.org

PETsMART Charities
19601 N. 27th Avenue
Phoenix, AZ 85027
602-580-6100

Spay USA
800-248-SPAY

United Kennel Club
100 E. Kilgore Road
Kalamazoo. MI 49002-5584
616-343-9020
http://www.ukcdogs.com

United States Dog Agility Association
P.O. Box 850995
Richardson, TX 75085-0955
972-231-9700
http:www.usdaa.com

Magazines

AKA *Gazette* - The American Kennel Club
260 Madison Avenue
New York, NY 10010
919-233-9767
http:www.akc.org/text/gazet.htm

ASPCA *Animal Watch* - The American
Society for the Prevention of Cruelty To
Animals
424 E. 92nd Street
New York, NY 10128-6804
212-876-7700
http://www.aspca.org

Animal Fair - Animal Fair Media
233 Park Avenue South, 6th Floor
New York, NY 10003
www.animalfair.com

Animals - Massachusetts Society for the
Prevention of Cruelty to Animals
800-998-0797

The Bark
2810 8th Street
Berkeley, CA 94710
510-704-0827

Dog Fancy- Fancy Publications
P.O. Box 53264
Boulder, CO 80322-3264
800-365-4421
http://www.dogfancy.com

Doggone
P.O. Box 65155
Vero Beach, FL 32965-1155
http://www.doggonefun.com

DOGS *Quarterly* - t.f.h. Publications, Inc.
P.O. Box 427
Neptune, NJ 07753-0427
732-988-8400
www.tfh.com

Dog World - Primedia
P.O. Box 56240
Boulder, CO 80322-6240
800-361-8056
http://www.dogworldmag.com

Good Dog! - Good Communications
P.O. Box 10069
Austin, TX 78766-1069
512-454-6090
gooddogmagazine.com

PetLife
1-800-767-9377

Pets: Part of the Family - Rodale Press
P.O. Box 7720
Red Oak, IA 51591-0720
In US and Canada - 888-721-7387
www.petspartofthefamily.com

Web Sites

To help you select the pet that is right for you
www.puppyfinder.com
www.selectsmart.com

To help you pick the perfect name for your pet
www.bowwow.com/au
www.petrix.com/dognames

Pictures and stories
www.baddogs.com

Show dog information
www.canismajor.com/dog

Virtual pet information
virtualpet.com/vp/index.htm.

Pet clothing catalogs

NMpet 800-825-8000
George 877-344-5454
Trixie & Peanut - 888-838-6780
Wagwear - 888-924-9327 or
www.wagwear.com

Stores

www.pets.com
www.Petopia.com
www.jcpenneypetclub.com

• Index •

About the Author

L isa Mendoza is an Emmy-winning journalist who worked in T.V. news for seventeen years. She's been named one of America's Top 100 Hispanic Women in Communications and has extensively researched the canine world for almost ten years. She is presently working on a line of children's books that explains the differences between such things as dog fur and human hair, canine and human teeth, and the canine and human digestive systems.

Photo Credits

Front cover: Elena Eaton, p. 2: Chris M. Mittelstead, p. 6: Lyn Snow, p. 9: Teresina Martin, p. 14: Sarah Boyd, p. 22: Alma Hansen, p. 43: Steven & Sharon Lark, p. 46: Trosper A. Parker, p. 50: Linda Meacham, p. 52: Ron Parenti, p. 55: Elena Eaton, p. 68: Bobbi Anderson, p. 70: Rodney E. Delara, p. 73: David Robert Crow, p. 75: Jennifer O'Rourke, p. 79: Marjorie Peters, p. 80: Sandy K. Medley, p. 84: Sandy Minter, p. 93: Alice Strange

Color Plates: 1-Middle: Darcy Matlock, 2-Top: Joy Thompson, 3-Top: Ann Huie, 3-Bottom: Christine Fennell, 5-Top: photo courtesy of *The Fresno Bee*, 5-Bottom, right: Teresina Martin, 6-Middle: Shelia Kincade, 7-Middle: Lori Reilly, 8-Top: Lee Anne Lysdahl

All other photos (color plates and back cover): copyright of Corel Corporation

Author photo (back dustjacket flap): Jose Garza Photography